"This series is a tremendous resource for those wanting to study and teach the Bible with an understanding of how the gospel is woven throughout Scripture. Here are gospel-minded pastors and scholars doing gospel business from all the Scriptures. This is a biblical and theological feast preparing God's people to apply the entire Bible to all of life with heart and mind wholly committed to Christ's priorities."

> **BRYAN CHAPELL,** President Emeritus, Covenant Theological Seminary; Senior Pastor, Grace Presbyterian Church, Peoria, Illinois

"Mark Twain may have smiled when he wrote to a friend, 'I didn't have time to write you a short letter, so I wrote you a long letter.' But the truth of Twain's remark remains serious and universal, because well-reasoned, compact writing requires extra time and extra hard work. And this is what we have in the Crossway Bible study series *Knowing the Bible*. The skilled authors and notable editors provide the contours of each book of the Bible as well as the grand theological themes that bind them together as one Book. Here, in a 12-week format, are carefully wrought studies that will ignite the mind and the heart."

> **R. KENT HUGHES,** Visiting Professor of Practical Theology, Westminster Theological Seminary

"*Knowing the Bible* brings together a gifted team of Bible teachers to produce a high-quality series of study guides. The coordinated focus of these materials is unique: biblical content, provocative questions, systematic theology, practical application, and the gospel story of God's grace presented all the way through Scripture."

> **PHILIP G. RYKEN,** President, Wheaton College

"These *Knowing the Bible* volumes provide a significant and very welcome variation on the general run of inductive Bible studies. This series provides substantial instruction, as well as teaching through the very questions that are asked. *Knowing the Bible* then goes even further by showing how any given text links with the gospel, the whole Bible, and the formation of theology. I heartily endorse this orientation of individual books to the whole Bible and the gospel, and I applaud the demonstration that sound theology was not something invented later by Christians, but is right there in the pages of Scripture."

> **GRAEME L. GOLDSWORTHY,** former lecturer, Moore Theological College; author, *According to Plan, Gospel and Kingdom, The Gospel in Revelation,* and *Gospel and Wisdom*

"What a gift to earnest, Bible-loving, Bible-searching believers! The organization and structure of the Bible study format presented through the *Knowing the Bible* series is so well conceived. Students of the Word are led to understand the content of passages through perceptive, guided questions, and they are given rich insights and application all along the way in the brief but illuminating sections that conclude each study. What potential growth in depth and breadth of understanding these studies offer! One can only pray that vast numbers of believers will discover more of God and the beauty of his Word through these rich studies."

> **BRUCE A. WARE,** Professor of Christian Theology, The Southern Baptist Theological Seminary

# KNOWING THE BIBLE

J. I. Packer, Theological Editor
Dane C. Ortlund, Series Editor
Lane T. Dennis, Executive Editor

• • • • • •

| | | | |
|---|---|---|---|
| Genesis | Psalms | Jonah, Micah, and Nahum | Ephesians |
| Exodus | Proverbs | | Philippians |
| Leviticus | Ecclesiastes | Haggai, Zechariah, and Malachi | Colossians and Philemon |
| Numbers | Song of Solomon | | |
| Deuteronomy | Isaiah | Matthew | 1–2 Thessalonians |
| Joshua | Jeremiah | Mark | 1–2 Timothy and Titus |
| Judges | Lamentations, Habakkuk, and Zephaniah | Luke | |
| Ruth and Esther | | John | |
| 1–2 Samuel | | Acts | Hebrews |
| 1–2 Kings | Ezekiel | Romans | James |
| 1–2 Chronicles | Daniel | 1 Corinthians | 1–2 Peter and Jude |
| Ezra and Nehemiah | Hosea | 2 Corinthians | 1–3 John |
| Job | Joel, Amos, and Obadiah | Galatians | Revelation |

• • • • • •

**J. I. PACKER** is Board of Governors' Professor of Theology at Regent College (Vancouver, BC). Dr. Packer earned his DPhil at the University of Oxford. He is known and loved worldwide as the author of the best-selling book Knowing God, as well as many other titles on theology and the Christian life. He serves as the General Editor of the ESV Bible and as the Theological Editor for the ESV Study Bible.

**LANE T. DENNIS** is President of Crossway, a not-for-profit publishing ministry. Dr. Dennis earned his PhD from Northwestern University. He is Chair of the ESV Bible Translation Oversight Committee and Executive Editor of the ESV Study Bible.

**DANE C. ORTLUND** is Executive Vice President of Bible Publishing and Bible Publisher at Crossway. He is a graduate of Covenant Theological Seminary (MDiv, ThM) and Wheaton College (BA, PhD). Dr. Ortlund has authored several books and scholarly articles in the areas of Bible, theology, and Christian living.

# MATTHEW

## A 12-WEEK STUDY

Drew Hunter

**CROSSWAY**®

WHEATON, ILLINOIS

Crossway is a publishing ministry of Good News Publishers.

| VP | | 28 | 27 | 26 | 25 | 24 | 23 | 22 | 21 | 20 | 19 | 18 |
|---|---|---|---|---|---|---|---|---|---|---|---|---|
| 16 | 15 | 14 | 13 | 12 | 11 | 10 | 9 | 8 | 7 | 6 | 5 | 4 |

# TABLE OF CONTENTS

# SERIES PREFACE

**KNOWING THE BIBLE**, as the series title indicates, was created to help readers know and understand the meaning, the message, and the God of the Bible. Each volume in the series consists of 12 units that progressively take the reader through a clear, concise study of that book of the Bible. In this way, any given volume can fruitfully be used in a 12-week format either in group study, such as in a church-based context, or in individual study. Of course, these 12 studies could be completed in fewer or more than 12 weeks, as convenient, depending on the context in which they are used.

Each study unit gives an overview of the text at hand before digging into it with a series of questions for reflection or discussion. The unit then concludes by highlighting the gospel of grace in each passage ("Gospel Glimpses"), identifying whole-Bible themes that occur in the passage ("Whole-Bible Connections"), and pinpointing Christian doctrines that are affirmed in the passage ("Theological Soundings").

The final component to each unit is a section for reflecting on personal and practical implications from the passage at hand. The layout provides space for recording responses to the questions proposed, and we think readers need to do this to get the full benefit of the exercise. The series also includes definitions of key words. These definitions are indicated by a note number in the text and are found at the end of each chapter.

Lastly, to help understand the Bible in this deeper way, we urge readers to use the ESV Bible and the *ESV Study Bible*, which are available in various print and digital formats, including online editions at esv.org. The Knowing the Bible series is also available online.

May the Lord greatly bless your study as you seek to know him through knowing his Word.

J. I. Packer
Lane T. Dennis

# WEEK 1: OVERVIEW

## Getting Acquainted

Matthew's account of the gospel is placed first among the other New Testament books and was one of the most popular books in the early church. It presents a clear and thorough account of who Jesus is and what he accomplished in his life, death, and resurrection. At the heart of Matthew's account is the identification of Jesus Christ as the true King of the universe who ushers in the kingdom of heaven. Matthew's Gospel also gives us a clear picture of discipleship,[1] with all of Jesus' radical demands on his followers amid a hostile world.

While each of the four Gospels draws attention to how Jesus fulfills the Old Testament, Matthew's account is the most explicitly and thoroughly Jewish. Additionally, while Matthew shares a lot of the same material with Mark and Luke, he organizes the material somewhat differently. While there is a broad chronological progression to Matthew's Gospel, he intentionally groups various teachings and events together in order to create a more "thematic" presentation.

## Placing It in the Larger Story

The story of the Bible is the story of the world. Beginning with the goodness of creation (Genesis 1–2), it soon progresses to humanity's rejection of God and the subsequent curse of this world (Genesis 3). The Old Testament is largely focused on the development of God's promise to reconcile[2] sinners to himself and restore all that is broken. The Old Testament ends in the middle of this story, longing for a resolution and the fulfillment of this promise.

In their own unique way, each of the four Gospels demonstrates that Jesus fulfills these profound, ancient longings. Matthew's Gospel is the one most explicitly focused on how Jesus is the long-awaited King who came to restore the goodness of creation by bringing in God's kingdom. This long-awaited restoration is . . .

- announced in Jesus' words as he declared, "Repent, for the kingdom of heaven is at hand" (Matt. 4:17).
- pictured in Jesus' works as he healed the sick, gave sight to the blind, calmed storms, cast out demons, and restored people to God through the forgiveness of their sins.
- accomplished through Jesus' death and resurrection, for he came "to give his life as a ransom for many" (Matt. 20:28).
- promised to arrive in its fullness in the coming "new world, when the Son of Man will sit on his glorious throne" (Matt. 19:28).

Looking backward, Matthew picks up the storyline of the Old Testament and shows how Jesus brings it to fulfillment in himself. Looking forward, Matthew ends his Gospel by propelling the church out into the world to take the gospel to all nations so that the reign of King Jesus is further expanded over all creation.

## Key Passage

"From that time Jesus began to preach, saying, 'Repent, for the kingdom of heaven is at hand'" (Matt. 4:17).

## Date and Historical Background

It appears that the author was Matthew (also known as Levi), a former tax collector who became one of the 12 disciples (see Matt. 9:9). Matthew probably wrote this account of the gospel in the late 50s or early 60s AD. Since he was a Galilean Jewish Christian, he knew the Old Testament Scriptures well and was thus able to interpret the words and actions of Jesus in light of the Old Testament storyline and promises.

The Gospel was likely written for a number of reasons and addressed to various types of people. With its topical breadth and orderly presentation of Christ's ministry, it becomes a basic course in discipleship for everyone who reads it, and clearly Matthew planned that it should. Because of the prevalence of Jewish themes, it was probably written with Jewish-Christians in particular in view.

For these Christians, Matthew's Gospel provides instruction about who Jesus is and his Jewish antecedents, how he fulfills the promises of the Old Testament, what he accomplished in his death and resurrection, and how to live as his people. This account would encourage them in their identity as the true people of God who follow the true King of the world. Judging by the ending of the book, one of Matthew's central purposes is also to encourage the church to be on mission, taking the gospel of Jesus Christ to the nations even amid great hostility.

## Outline

I. The Arrival in History of Jesus the Messiah (1:1–2:23)

II. John the Baptist Prepares for the Appearance of the Messianic Kingdom (3:1–17)

III. Jesus the Messiah Begins to Advance the Messianic Kingdom (4:1–25)

IV. The Authoritative Message of the Messiah: Kingdom Life for His Disciples (5:1–7:29)

V. The Authoritative Power of the Messiah: Kingdom Power Demonstrated (8:1–9:38)

VI. The Authoritative Mission of the Messiah's Messengers (10:1–42)

VII. Opposition to the Messiah Emerges (11:1–12:50)

VIII. Mysteries of the Messianic Kingdom Revealed in Parables (13:1–53)

IX. The Identity of the Messiah Revealed (13:54–16:20)

X. The Suffering of the Messiah Revealed (16:21–17:27)

XI. The Community of the Messiah Revealed (18:1–20:34)

XII. The Messiah Asserts His Authority over Jerusalem (21:1–23:39)

XIII. The Delay, Return, and Judgment of the Messiah (24:1–25:46)

XIV. The Crucified Messiah (26:1–27:66)

XV. The Resurrection and Commissioning Action of the Messiah (28:1–20)

## As You Get Started . . .

Read over the outline above and take several minutes to flip through the Gospel of Matthew, scanning its contents. What are a few things you expect this account of the gospel to highlight from the life and ministry of Jesus?

-------------------------------------------------------------------------------

-------------------------------------------------------------------------------

-------------------------------------------------------------------------------

Have you read through or studied the gospel of Matthew before? If so, what particular aspects are you looking forward to studying in more detail? If not, what are a few things you hope to better understand about Jesus?

After reading this introduction, what is your understanding of how Matthew's Gospel relates to the Old Testament?

From your previous reading of Matthew or your initial exposure in this study, are there aspects of this book that confuse you? Do you have any specific questions that you hope to have answered through this study?

## As You Finish This Unit . . .

In Matthew 4:4, Jesus says, "Man shall not live by bread alone, but by every word that comes from the mouth of God." Take a moment to ask God to speak to you through the book of Matthew, giving you fresh conviction, encouragement, and a transformed heart and life.

### Definitions

[1] **Disciple** – Any person who submits to the teachings of another. In the NT, the word refers to those who submitted themselves to the teaching of Jesus, especially those who traveled with him during his ministry.

[2] **Reconciliation** – The restoration of a positive relationship and peace between alienated or opposing parties. Through his death and resurrection, Jesus has reconciled believers to God (2 Cor. 5:18–21).

# WEEK 2: THE ARRIVAL OF JESUS THE MESSIAH

Matthew 1–2

## The Place of the Passage

The opening two chapters of Matthew announce the arrival in world history of Jesus Christ. This was a long-anticipated moment in an ongoing story. Through various Old Testament references, allusions, and quotations Matthew shows us that Jesus came as the climax of the Old Testament storyline. He is the long awaited Messiah,[1] the King who will bring to fulfillment God's promises to rescue his people and restore this broken world.

## The Big Picture

In Matthew 1–2 Jesus arrives as the long-awaited King who came to save his people from their sins.

> ## Reflection and Discussion

Read through the complete passage for this study, Matthew 1–2. Then think through and write your own notes on the following questions. (For further background, see the *ESV Study Bible*, pages 1820–1823, available online at esv.org.)

### 1. The Long-Awaited King Arrives (1:1–1:25)

From his titles (Matt. 1:1) to his genealogy (1:2–17), Matthew clearly situates Jesus within history in general and the Old Testament story in particular. How so?

--------

--------

--------

--------

By calling Jesus the "son of Abraham" and "son of David" (Matt. 1:1), Matthew gives us a concise yet thick description of Jesus' identity. Reflect on the central promises God gave to Abraham (see Gen. 12:1–3; 22:18) and David (see 2 Sam. 7:11–16; Ps. 89:3–4). What light do these shed on what Jesus came to do?

--------

--------

--------

--------

--------

Since ancient genealogies customarily traced lineage through men, the inclusion of five women—Tamar (Matt. 1:3), Rahab (v. 5), Ruth (v. 5), Bathsheba ("the wife of Uriah"; v. 6), and Mary (v. 16)—is unusual. Further, Tamar, Rahab, and Ruth were Gentiles (non-Jews), and Tamar, Rahab, and Bathsheba were women of questionable character. Why would Matthew draw attention to these aspects of Jesus' lineage? How does this already anticipate what we learn of Jesus in 1:21?

--------

--------

--------

--------

--------

What evidence is there that Matthew's presentation of Jesus' genealogy is very carefully structured? Identify the key moments or turning points in the ongoing story that is referenced through the genealogy.

When he heard that Mary was pregnant, Joseph naturally assumed that she had been unfaithful to him. Yet how did he respond (Matt. 1:18–19)? How did he change his actions after the angel visited him (vv. 20–24)? In what ways is Joseph portrayed as a model disciple (consider 9:13; 12:7)?

## 2. Initial Responses to the King (2:1–12)

The foreign wise men (or *magi*, i.e., magicians or astrologers) were likely familiar with Old Testament prophecies. How does Numbers 24:17 help us understand why they would follow a star to find a king? Additionally, read Psalm 72:8–11, 15, in the context of the whole psalm. How does this shed light on the wise men's actions in Matthew 2:11?

Isaiah 60:1–5 tells us that when a "light" comes to Israel it will be the time of salvation for his people and renewal for the world. This should cause the people's hearts to thrill and rejoice (Isa. 60:5). When this "light" finally comes, who ends up responding properly and who does not (note Matt. 2:3, 10)?

How do Herod's disposition, plotting, and actions in Matthew 2:3–8 and verse 16 already set our expectations for what is to come (see Matt. 26:3–4; 27:1–2)?

### 3. Flight and Return (2:13–23)

Review Exodus 1:15–22 and 2:11–15, then consider in what ways Herod's actions in Matthew 2:13–16 parallel those of the ancient king of Egypt.

Three times in Matthew 2:13–23 we hear that something happened to Jesus in order that the Old Testament might be "fulfilled" (2:15, 17–18, 23). What is Matthew trying to show us about the relationship between Old Testament expectations and the arrival of Jesus?

Read through the following three sections on *Gospel Glimpses, Whole-Bible Connections,* and *Theological Soundings*. Then take time to consider the *Personal Implications* these sections may have for you.

**COUNTERCULTURAL GRACE.** Matthew's genealogy presses firmly against his day's cultural impulses. First, while genealogies would typically include only men, Matthew mentions four women. Second, he doesn't go out of his way to include the noblest women in Jesus' line, such as Sarah, the great matriarch and wife of Abraham. Just the opposite. Tamar posed as a prostitute (Genesis 38), Rahab was a prostitute, and David made Bathsheba an adulterer. Third, Rahab and Ruth were Gentiles, and Bathsheba was married to a Gentile. Jesus' lineage runs against the first century's cultural instincts (by including women), moral instincts (by including *these* women), and religious instincts (by including non-Jews). Jesus didn't come for a particular gender, race, or type of sinner (see Gal. 3:29). Woven into the very lineage of our Savior are the diverse kinds of people he came to save.

**SAVED FROM SINS.** "Jesus" is the Greek name for the Hebrew "Joshua," which means, "Yahweh[2] saves." This name communicates what he came to do: "you shall call his name Jesus, for he will save his people from their sins" (Matt. 1:21). "Salvation" is often a comprehensive term for all the ways that God saves his people through the work of Jesus. Here in Matthew the focus is on being saved from our sins, for this is our deepest problem and most basic need. Jesus' name declares his commitment to rescue us from this root issue. And what is declared in his name was displayed in his death, for there he saves us by taking upon himself all our sins.

**A CONTINUING STORY.** Like a book with chapters, the Old Testament is a singular epic story that progresses from one shorter story to the next. This story begins with the creation of the world (Genesis 1–2), plunges into the fall[3] (Genesis 3), and rises with God's promise to make all things right again (Gen. 3:15; 12:1–3). According to the contours of Matthew's genealogy, the outworking of this promise begins with Abraham, progresses through kingship with David and exile into Babylon, and ends with an increased longing for the arrival of the Christ, or Messiah (Matt. 1:17). This opening to Matthew's Gospel is more than a list of names; it is a genealogical story wherein the history of Israel is reviewed and brought to its proper climax with Jesus Christ.

**THE PROMISED KING.** God promised David that one from his own line would rule forever over an everlasting kingdom (2 Sam. 7:12–13). While Israel's kingdom crumbled, the prophets kept the promise alive (Isa. 9:6–7; Jer. 33:17; Ezek. 34:23–24). After centuries of waiting, Matthew announces that this "son of David" has arrived (Matt. 1:1). He traces Jesus' lineage right through David, "the king" (1:6), and up to Joseph, another "son of David" (1:16, 20), who adopts Jesus into this royal line. As a consequence of his life, death, and resurrection, Jesus is already reigning as King, though we do not yet see the full manifestation of his rule that will occur when he returns.

**NEW EXODUS.** Matthew tells us Jesus' flight to Egypt and subsequent return occurred in order to fulfill what the Lord had spoken in Hosea 11:1: "Out of Egypt I called my son" (Matt. 2:15). This quotation from Hosea is not in itself, however, a future-looking prediction about Jesus, but a backward remembering of Israel when they, as God's "son" (see Ex. 4:22–23), were brought out from Egypt at the exodus.[4] If it's not a promise, how can it be fulfilled? When we read the quotation in its context, we find that Hosea isn't just thinking of the past exodus-event. He is looking forward to *another* exodus-like redemption for God's people (Hos. 2:14–15; 11:8–12, especially v. 11). Jesus arrives as the true "Son" of God, the true Israel. The exodus story is reenacted in Jesus' own life to show that he has come to fulfill Hosea's promise of a new and greater deliverance for those he saves. Jesus came to bring us out of our slavery to sin and Satan in order to restore us to God.

## Theological Soundings

**INCARNATION.** Mary "was found to be with child from the Holy Spirit" (Matt. 1:18). This is a great mystery. We call it the incarnation, which literally means "en-fleshing." In a singular moment of time, just over 2,000 years ago, the God who created all things entered into this creation and became a part of it. In Jesus Christ, God became a man. Jesus is not half-man and half-God, but he is truly man and truly God, and both, so to speak, in full. He is this human "child" inside of Mary, and yet he is also to be called "Immanuel," which means, "God with us" (1:23).

**ANGELS.** Angels, messengers of God, serve an important role in the events surrounding the earliest days of Jesus' life. As an angel (Gabriel) had announced Jesus' forthcoming birth to Mary, so angels appeared to Joseph when he was planning to break off his engagement with her (Matt. 1:20) and also before and after Herod plotted against Jesus' life (2:13, 19). The supernatural world of angels and demons is assumed and taught throughout the Bible. We see their active presence perhaps most often in the Gospel narratives.

## Personal Implications

Take time to think about and make notes on the personal implications for your own life today in the (1) *Gospel Glimpses*, (2) *Whole-Bible Connections*, (3) *Theological*

*Soundings*, and (4) this passage as a whole. Also consider what you have learned that might lead you to praise God, repent of sin, trust his gracious promises, and live in obedience to him.

## 1. Gospel Glimpses

## 2. Whole-Bible Connections

## 3. Theological Soundings

## 4. Matthew 1–2

▶ **As You Finish This Unit . . .**

Take a moment now to ask for the Lord's blessing and help as you continue in this study of Matthew. And take a moment also to look back through this unit of study, to reflect on a few key things that the Lord may be teaching you—and perhaps to highlight and underline these things to review again in the future.

### Definitions

[1] **Messiah** – Transliteration of a Hebrew word meaning "anointed one," the equivalent of the Greek word *Christ*. Originally applied to anyone specially designated for a particular role, such as king or priest. In Jesus' day, the term denoted Israel's promised deliverer-king Jesus himself affirmed that he was the Messiah sent from God (Matt. 16:16–17).

[2] **Yahweh** – The likely English form of the name represented by the Hebrew letters *YHWH*. The Lord revealed this unique name for himself to Moses at the burning bush and told him to instruct the Israelites to call on him by it (Exodus 3). English translations of the Bible usually render this term as "Lord," with small capital letters.

[3] **Fall, the** – Adam and Eve's disobedience to God by eating the fruit from the tree of the knowledge of good and evil, resulting in their loss of innocence and favor with God and the introduction of sin and its effects into the world (Genesis 3; Rom. 5:12–21; 1 Cor. 15:21–22).

[4] **Exodus** – The departure of the people of Israel from Egypt and their journey to Mount Sinai under Moses' leadership, en route for the Promised Land (Exodus 1–19).

# Week 3: Jesus Prepares for Ministry and Announces the Kingdom

Matthew 3–4

At least 25 years have passed since Joseph and his family moved back to Nazareth. The focus therefore immediately shifts from Jesus' arrival and infancy in Matthew 1–2 to the beginning of his public ministry in Matthew 3–4. John the Baptist introduces the arrival of Jesus and, with him, the arrival of the kingdom of heaven. Before Jesus begins his public ministry, however, he will first be identified as God's Son through his baptism[1] and will successfully resist temptation.

## The Big Picture

After John the Baptist announces the arrival of the kingdom of heaven, Jesus is baptized, endures through temptation, and calls his first disciples.

## Reflection and Discussion

**Read through the complete passage for this study, Matthew 3–4. Then review the questions below concerning this section of Matthew's Gospel and write your notes on them. (For further background, see the *ESV Study Bible*, pages 1824–1827, available online at esv.org.)**

### 1. John the Baptist Prepares for the Arrival of the Kingdom (3:1–17)

All four Gospels quote Isaiah 40:3 with reference to John the Baptist's ministry (Matt. 3:3; Mark 1:2–3; Luke 3:4–6; John 1:23). Isaiah prophesied that a messenger would be sent to proclaim that God himself was about to return to his exiled[2] people, Israel. Whose entrance does John end up announcing? What does this tell us about Jesus' identity?

The promises of Malachi 3:1 and 4:5–6 are similar to those of Isaiah 40:3. They prophesied the return of the prophet Elijah (i.e., one like Elijah) to prepare the way for God's arrival to save and judge. How might the strange description of John in Matthew 3:4 link him with these promises (see 2 Kings 1:8)?

How are people to respond to the news of the nearness of God's kingdom-rule (Matt. 3:2, 6, 8)? Why is it so urgent (see vv. 10–12)?

<br>
<br>
<br>
<br>
<br>
<br>

For the reader who reflects on Old Testament allusions, Jesus' baptism is thick with implications for understanding his identity and mission. Read Isaiah 42:1; 61:1; and 2 Samuel 7:12–14 in their respective contexts (see also Ps. 2:6–7). Note any parallels with Matthew 3:16–17. What does this tell us about Jesus' unique identity?

<br>
<br>
<br>
<br>
<br>
<br>

## 2. The Victory of Jesus in Temptation (4:1–11)

Jesus' 40 days of testing in the wilderness corresponds to Israel's 40 years of testing in the wilderness (Deut. 8:2–3). How did Israel, God's national "son," fare in their repeated testing? How did Jesus, God's "beloved Son" (Matt. 3:17) do when tested himself?

<br>
<br>
<br>
<br>
<br>

What does Jesus' response to the first temptation in Matthew 3:4 tell us about the importance of God's Word for our lives? Notice also that Jesus quotes Scripture (presumably from memory) to Satan amid each temptation (Matt.

4:4, 7, 10). What do we learn here about the importance of God's Word for enduring temptation?

### 3. Jesus Begins His Ministry (4:12–25)

Jesus intentionally began his ministry in Galilee, the land of Gentiles (Matt. 4:12–15). How does this connect with what we learned about certain women in Jesus' genealogy? How does this link up with his commission to his disciples in Matthew 28:19?

With the command to "follow me," Jesus gives us a primary way of describing what it means to be his disciple. He then defines this in terms of evangelistic mission: "and I will make you fishers of men" (v. 19; see also Matt. 28:19). Note two or three practical things you can do in your life to follow Jesus as a missionary disciple.

Matthew 4:23–24 summarizes Jesus' ministry. What are the three primary things Jesus does? How do Jesus' actions demonstrate the reality that the king-dom of heaven is at hand, that is, that God is restoring this broken world?

Read through the following three sections on *Gospel Glimpses, Whole-Bible Connections*, and *Theological Soundings*. Then take time to consider the *Personal Implications* these sections may have for you.

## Gospel Glimpses

**A GRACIOUS DELAY.** John the Baptist's message is ominous. "Even now," he says, "the axe is laid at the root of the trees. Every tree therefore that does not bear good fruit is cut down and thrown into the fire" (Matt. 3:10; see v. 12). This is a strong warning of imminent judgment. Yet when Jesus arrives, bless-ing is unleashed and judgment is delayed. Why? To magnify God's patience, for "the Lord is not slow to fulfill his promise as some count slowness, but is patient toward you, not wishing that any should perish, but that all should reach repentance" (2 Pet. 3:9).

**TEMPTED LIKE US AND FOR US.** Jesus' endurance through temptation is not primarily an example to follow but a victory to rejoice in. When Adam and Eve were tempted, they failed. When Israel was tempted, they failed. Often when we are tempted, we fail. But here is "one who in every respect has been tempted as we are, yet without sin" (Heb. 4:15). Jesus Christ is the only one in all of history to stand firm. He did it because we didn't. Jesus lived the perfect life we failed to live and died the guilty death we deserve to die. Now any of us moral failures can receive his perfect record in place of our own. We now seek to follow Jesus' example not in order to become righteous, but because Jesus' obedience and sacrifice has already made us so.

## Whole-Bible Connections

**TRUE ISRAEL.** Through his geographic movements and actions Jesus repeats the story of Israel, recapitulating Israel's exodus in his own experience. Israel was called out of Egypt as God's national "son" (Ex. 4:22–23), passed through the Red Sea (which was interpreted as a baptism; see 1 Cor. 10:1–2), and entered the wilderness for 40 years of testing (Num. 14:34). Like Israel before, Jesus was called out of Egypt as God's son (Matt. 2:15; quoting Hosea 11:1), passed through the Jordan River in baptism (Matt. 3:1–16), and entered the wilderness for 40 days of testing (Matt. 4:1–11). Matthew shows us that Jesus is the true Israel, repeating Israel's story in his own life. However, this Israel is truly obedient, succeeding where the first one failed.

**KINGDOM OF HEAVEN.** John and Jesus both announce the near arrival of God's kingdom with the same words, "the kingdom of heaven is at hand" (Matt. 3:2; 4:17). Although this exact phrase is not found in the Old Testament, the idea is there from the beginning. God created humanity in his image so that they would reflect his rule as they "have dominion" over the whole world (Gen. 1:26, 28). But rather than submitting to God and exercising authority over the serpent, they committed cosmic treason (Gen. 3:1–7). The kingdom of Eden fell and the serpent—Satan—took the throne (see John 12:31; 14:30; 16:11). God is still the ultimate King, but his rule is no longer recognized and the world is enemy-occupied territory. The subsequent story of the Old Testament is the outworking of God's plan to reestablish his kingdom. This plan progresses through the establishment of the kingdom of Israel with their line of Davidic kings (see Gen. 17:6; 49:9–10; Ex. 19:6; 2 Sam. 7:12–14). Yet the glory of this kingdom fades and God's people are left longing for him to return to reestablish his rule (Isa. 52:7). With the arrival of Jesus, this kingdom has dawned.

**END OF EXILE.** Jesus' baptism answers an ancient prayer. At the moment when Jesus came out of the water, the heavens were opened and the Spirit of God descended (Matt. 3:16). In Isaiah 64:1, Israel cried out, "Oh that you would rend the heavens and come down." They felt themselves in exile away from their land and away from God, pleading with him to rescue them once again as he did at the exodus (Isa. 63:11–64:3). By asking God to open the heavens and come down, they pleaded with him to return to them and end their exile. After hundreds of years of silence, the heavens opened and God's presence came down. Through Jesus, God declares that the exile is over and people are welcomed back into his presence through faith.

## ▶ Theological Soundings

**TRINITY.** The Bible teaches that there is one God who eternally exists as three persons—Father, Son, and Holy Spirit. All three persons of the Trinity are present at Jesus' baptism. The Son is baptized, the Spirit descends in the form of a dove, and the Father speaks from heaven (Matt. 3:16–17). All three persons of the Trinity are actively engaged in the process of saving sinners. Broadly speaking, the Father plans salvation from eternity past, the Son accomplishes it on the cross, and the Spirit applies it throughout the ages.

REPENTANCE. The arrival of the kingdom of heaven calls for a response of "repentance" (Matt. 3:2; 4:17). Repentance refers to a radical reorientation of life. It refers to the turning of one's mind, heart, and will *away* from sin and *toward* God in faith. With this reorientation of the deepest affections of our hearts, our thoughts and actions will also begin to change. In John's words, we must and shall "bear fruit in keeping with repentance" (Matt. 3:8).

## Personal Implications

Take time to reflect on and make notes on the personal implications of Matthew for your own life today regarding the (1) *Gospel Glimpses*, (2) *Whole-Bible Connections*, (3) *Theological Soundings*, and (4) this passage as a whole. Also consider what you have learned that might lead you to praise God, repent of sin, trust his gracious promises, and live in obedience to him.

### 1. Gospel Glimpses

### 2. Whole-Bible Connections

### 3. Theological Soundings

## 4. Matthew 3–4

---
---
---
---
---
---

> ## As You Finish This Unit . . .

Take a moment now to ask for the Lord's blessing and help as you continue in this study of Matthew. And take a moment also to look back through this unit of study, to reflect on a few key things that the Lord may be teaching you—and perhaps to highlight and underline these things to review again in the future.

### Definitions

[1] **Baptism** – To baptize is literally "to immerse," or "to wash." Refers to the Christian practice of a new believer passing under water as an outward sign of the inward reality of regeneration through union with Christ in his death and resurrection.

[2] **Exile** – Several relocations of large groups of Israelites/Jews have occurred throughout history, but "the exile" typically refers to God's judgment of Israel through the relocation of residents of the southern kingdom of Judah to Babylon in 586 BC.

# WEEK 4: JESUS' AUTHORITATIVE MESSAGE

Matthew 5–7

## The Place of the Passage

Matthew 4:23–24 shows the two things that mark Jesus' ministry: his words and his works. He taught and proclaimed the gospel (his words), and he also healed people and cast out demons (his works). Matthew 5–7 focuses on the first of these two aspects. Jesus' authority is displayed through his teaching in what has come to be known as the "Sermon on the Mount." In this compact section we hear Jesus' radical call to humble, heart-level, non-hypocritical, faith-filled, single-minded commitment to Jesus and his ways.

## The Big Picture

Matthew 5–7 presents Jesus' authoritative teaching on the faith-filled, obedient life of discipleship.

> ## Reflection and Discussion

Read through the complete passage for this study, Matthew 5–7. Then think through and write your own notes on the following questions. (For further background, see the *ESV Study Bible*, pages 1827–1835, available online at esv.org.)

### 1. The Counterculture of the Kingdom (5:1–16)

The opening verses give a portrait of a true disciple of Jesus (Matt. 5:2–12). These statements are pronouncements of blessing, celebration, and affirmation over those who fit the description. How are these descriptions in stark contrast to the characteristics celebrated in your culture? Note two or three things you can do to cultivate these character traits in your own life. Additionally, jot down a couple of ways you can affirm these in the lives of others.

Though persecuted by the world around them (Matt. 5:10–12), Jesus' disciples must have an actively positive presence in this world. Salt was known as a beneficial preservative for meat, and light shines in the darkness (Matt. 5:13–16). List three examples of what it looks like to be a community of salt and light in the world. What do you think is a primary way that Christians are tempted to hide their light?

### 2. Kingdom Obedience and the Old Testament (5:17–7:12)

Matthew 5:17–20 describes how the new age of the kingdom has both continuity and discontinuity with the era of the Old Testament. In what ways does

Jesus emphasize the ongoing importance of the Old Testament? How does he imply that the Old Testament is brought to completion in him and his kingdom?

In Matthew 5:21–48, Jesus gives six examples of what it means for disciples to live according to the Old Testament law's fulfillment and to have an obedience greater than that of the leaders of his day (see Matt. 5:17–20). These examples involve such things as anger (5:21–26), lust (5:27–30), divorce (5:31–32), and how we treat others (5:43–48). In order to crystalize what this radical, heart-level obedience looks like in everyday life, write a one-sentence summary of each example.

According to Matthew 6:1–18, what are the different means whereby people might express their faith in a hypocritical way (see also Matt. 23:5, 25–28)? Where do you see religious hypocrisy[1] today? What truth does Jesus repeat throughout this section as a motivation for a non-hypocritical faith?

What does our attitude about money and possessions reveal about our values and loyalties in life (Matt. 6:19–24)? How does Jesus show anxiety to be ultimately a faith issue, that is, an issue of how firmly we trust that God is our Father (6:25–34)?

In what sense are we not to judge others, according to Matthew 7:1–5? Is Jesus forbidding all evaluation or even forming an opinion about others (see v. 5)? How does verse 6 imply that we must judge others in some sense? What then is the deeper heart-attitude that Jesus is condemning?

What does Matthew 7:7–11 teach us about God's character, and how is this an encouragement to be prayerful?

## 3. Two Ways to Live (7:13–29)

Jesus concludes by contrasting two pathways that lead to two destinies: the wide gate and easy path that leads to destruction, and the narrow gate that leads to life (Matt. 7:13–14). It is obvious that the "wide road" is the pathway of the irreligious and blatantly disobedient. But note 7:15, 21–23. What do you see here that indicates that this path will also be filled with religious people who only *appear* to know and follow Jesus?

What are the various ways that Matthew 7:15–27 describes the path of radical, wholehearted obedience?

---

Read through the following three sections on *Gospel Glimpses, Whole-Bible Connections*, and *Theological Soundings*. Then take time to consider the *Personal Implications* these sections may have for you.

## Gospel Glimpses

**POOR IN SPIRIT.** The first beatitude celebrates "the poor in spirit," not the spiritual elite (Matt. 5:3). Jesus' kingdom is for those who know they don't deserve it, for those who admit their spiritual impoverishment. When a man goes financially bankrupt in this life, he may lose everything. But when one admits spiritual bankruptcy before God, he gains everything. In Jesus' kingdom economy, it's only when we admit we have nothing that we inherit everything.

**GOD, OUR FATHER.** Jesus referred to God as a father 17 times throughout the Sermon on the Mount. As our Father, God graciously and generously forgives us (Matt. 6:14), rewards us (6:4, 6, 18), provides for us (6:26, 32), and responds to our requests (7:11). As his children, we are called to imitate his love (5:43–48), pray to him (6:9), and trust him (6:25–34). This is a wondrous gospel privilege, for it is through Jesus' work on the cross that we receive our adoption into God's family (John 1:12–13; Gal. 3:26; 4:4–5). All who come to

31

the Father through Jesus Christ enjoy his irrevocable fatherly affection in place of his wrath. Deserving to flee as enemies, we boldly draw near as children. This is at the heart of what it means to be a Christian.

**IMPOSSIBLE OBEDIENCE MADE POSSIBLE.** There can be no honest reading of Jesus' words that overlooks his radical demands. "Unless your righteousness exceeds that of the scribes and Pharisees, you will never enter the kingdom of heaven," he says (Matt. 5:20). As he explains, his commands cannot be externally managed; they must be obeyed from the heart (5:21–48). When his disciples later wondered how this kind of obedience is possible, Jesus responds, "with man this is impossible, but with God all things are possible" (19:26). In other words, God is the one who makes this kind of obedience achievable. Jesus must empower the very obedience he demands. And he does. He gave this sermon on his way to the cross where he would inaugurate the new covenant (26:28), which not only would bring us forgiveness for our failures, but would give us new hearts and the Spirit's empowerment to obey (26:28; see Ezek. 36:26–27; Jer. 31:33). These radical demands come with radical gifts.

## Whole-Bible Connections

**FULFILLMENT OF THE LAW AND THE PROPHETS.** Jesus says, "Do not think that I have come to abolish the Law or the Prophets" (Matt. 5:17). He did not come to simply reestablish the authority of the Law[2] and the Prophets, for he does not contrast "abolish" with "teach" or "reaffirm." "I have not come to abolish them," he says, "but to *fulfill* them." Jesus did not come to do away with the Scriptures but to bring them to their appointed goal. The Old Testament is a story that finds its resolution in Jesus. The tip of the Old Testament arrow rests directly on him. Or, as Jesus said elsewhere, "everything written about me in the Law of Moses and the Prophets and the Psalms must be fulfilled" (Luke 24:44; see also John 5:39, 46).

**THE HONOR OF HIS NAME.** The first request of the Lord's Prayer is, "hallowed be your name" (Matt. 6:9). This is not a statement of praise, but a plea. It is a request that God would cause his name to be honored (lit., "sanctify your name"). It is a request that rises out of the pages of the Old Testament. When Israel was scattered in exile among the nations, their continued disobedience dishonored God's name. "But I had concern for my holy name," God says, "which the house of Israel had profaned among the nations to which they came" (Ezek. 36:21). Then God announces how he will act "for the sake of [His] holy name" (v. 22). "I will cleanse you. And I will give you a new heart. . . . And I will put my Spirit within you, and cause you to walk in my statutes and be careful to obey my rules" (vv. 25b–27). God will cause his name to be honored by creating a people who receive his grace and are radically transformed to obey his word. According to Jesus, this should be our first prayer—that God would change people so that they would receive his grace and honor him with all their hearts.

## Theological Soundings

**EVIL NATURE.** "If you then, who are evil, know how to give good gifts to your children . . ." (Matt. 7:11). Jesus affirms his hearers' good parental dispositions to care for their children. He also affirms their evil nature. Both are true. As humans made in God's image, we all will reflect his good character in varying degrees. But ever since the fall of humanity, all humans except Jesus have had, and displayed, impure, distorted motives and dispositions. We are often very nice people. But we're also evil. The Bible affirms that we are all sinful and broken, in need of healing and restoration.

**HELL.** Some of Jesus' more difficult statements—not difficult to understand, but difficult to accept—are his warnings of judgment. Jesus warned that those who don't fight sin will be "thrown into hell" (Matt. 5:29–30). The word used for "hell" is *gehenna*, which was the trash heap near the city that was regularly set on fire. According to Jesus, hell is the place of "destruction" (7:13), "eternal fire" (25:41), and "eternal punishment" (25:46). It is a place of terrible suffering where there will be "weeping and gnashing of teeth" (8:12; 13:42, 50; 22:13; 24:51; 25:30). That Jesus often spoke about hell does not diminish his love but demonstrates it. He spoke about hell because he didn't want people to go there. Indeed, when he spoke of hell, he was also speaking of what he would experience on the cross in the place of sinners who deserve to go there.

## Personal Implications

Take time to think about and make notes on the personal implications of Matthew for your own life today regarding the (1) *Gospel Glimpses*, (2) *Whole-Bible Connections*, (3) *Theological Soundings*, and (4) this passage as a whole. Also consider what you have learned that might lead you to praise God, repent of sin, trust his gracious promises, and live in obedience to him.

### 1. Gospel Glimpses

## 2. Whole-Bible Connections

## 3. Theological Soundings

## 4. Matthew 5–7

▶ **As You Finish This Unit . . .**

Take a moment now to ask for the Lord's blessing and help as you continue in this study of Matthew. And take a moment also to look back through this unit of study, to reflect on a few key things that the Lord may be teaching you—and perhaps to highlight and underline these things to review again in the future.

### Definitions

[1] **Hypocrisy** – Presenting oneself falsely to others in order to gain positive regard or praise. Derived from Greek for "actor."

[2] **Law, the** – When spelled with an initial capital letter, "Law" refers to the first five books of the Bible. When spelled with all lowercase letters ("law"), it refers to the entire body of precepts set forth in the books of the Law. The law contains numerous commands of God to his people, including the Ten Commandments and instructions regarding worship, sacrifice, and life in Israel.

# WEEK 5: JESUS' AUTHORITATIVE MINISTRY AND EXTENDED MISSION

Matthew 8–10

▲

Matthew 4:23 and 9:35 serve as bookends for everything in between. They summarize Jesus' ministry as "teaching in their synagogues and proclaiming the gospel of the kingdom and healing every disease and every affliction." This presents Jesus' twofold ministry as teaching/preaching and healing/restoring. Between these two statements Matthew thematically organizes his material to show both aspects in turn. Having just demonstrated Jesus' teaching ministry in chapters 5–7, Matthew now turns to Jesus' ministry of healing and restoration in chapters 8–9. Jesus multiplies his ministry in chapter 10 by sending his disciples to continue this twofold ministry elsewhere.

WEEK 5: JESUS' AUTHORITATIVE MINISTRY AND EXTENDED MISSION

## The Big Picture

In chapters 8–10 Jesus brings his healing power to the world and multiplies his ministry by sending his disciples to participate in his mission.

## Reflection and Discussion

Read through the complete passage for this study, Matthew 8–10. Then review the questions below concerning this section of Matthew's Gospel and write your notes on them. (For further background, see the *ESV Study Bible*, pages 1835–1842, available online at esv.org.)

### 1. Demonstration of Jesus' Authoritative Power (8:1–9:35)

The Old Testament gave specific guidelines for the treatment of those with various skin diseases, generically called leprosy (see Leviticus 13–14). To touch a leper would make one ceremonially unclean (Num. 19:11–21). But what happens when Jesus touches this leper (Matt. 8:2–3)? Furthermore, Jesus tells the man to show himself to the priest, which was the first step toward returning to society. What does this show us about Jesus' compassion?

Matthew shows Jesus' authority in action throughout chapters 8–9. He cast out demons "with a word" (8:16; seen in action in v. 32), "rebuked" the winds and sea into obedience (8:26–27), and displayed his "authority on earth to forgive sins" (9:6). In what ways does Jesus' interaction with the Roman officer in Matthew 8:5–13 emphasize this authority from the outset?

"I will follow you wherever you go" (Matt. 8:19). This is the unqualified profession of a true disciple. Yet reflect on Matthew 8:20–22 and how following Jesus involves a new set of priorities and expectations for this life. This would-be disciple asks to "let me first go and bury my father" (who apparently was not yet deceased). Write an example of what a modern would-be disciple might say to Jesus today. According to the kind of response Jesus gave in verse 22, write also how you imagine Jesus would respond to this modern would-be disciple.

After Jesus calmed the natural world's chaos (Matt. 8:23–27), the demons recognized that he would also overpower the chaos of the spiritual world (see v. 29). How does the pigs' fate in the sea prefigure the final fate of demons[1] (compare Matt. 8:30–32 with Rev. 20:10)? What often-neglected aspect of Jesus' mission does this highlight?

Judging by the reaction of the scribes to Jesus' proclamation of forgiveness in Matthew 9:3, who is Jesus demonstrating himself to be (see also Mark 2:7)?

Jesus said he came not for the healthy, but the sick; not for the righteous, but sinners (Matt. 9:12–13). Of course, no one is righteous on their own (see Rom. 3:10ff.). Jesus came for those who have enough honest self-awareness to admit their spiritual need. What is the implication for how we should view ourselves? How would you characterize the Pharisees'[2] self-understanding?

---

A ruler recently suffered the death of his daughter (Matt. 9:18), a woman suffered 12 years of social marginalization due to her condition (v. 20), and two men suffer from blindness (v. 27). How, specifically, does Matthew present the faith of each of them (see v. 18 for the ruler, v. 21 for the woman, and v. 28 for the blind men)? How does Jesus respond to each one? Why (see vv. 22, 29)?

---

## 2. Extension of Jesus' Mission (9:36–10:42)

Some have noted that the disciples' mission is essentially an extension of Jesus' own mission. What do you see in Matthew 10:1, 7–8 that confirms this conclusion when read in light of what we've already seen in Matthew (note especially 4:17, 23; 9:35, and the events of Matthew 8–9)?

---

It seems that the disciples' immediate short-term missionary journey through Israel (Matt. 10:5–15) provides the context for Jesus to teach about their future mission into the broader world when he's gone (10:16–42). Read verses 16–22, 34–36 and note what kinds of persecution will accompany the church's mission. How do you see this in the world today?

Abandoning Jesus because of persecution is simply not an option, for only "the one who endures to the end will be saved" (Matt. 10:22). Jesus gives numerous motivations to endure with firm, fearless, even joyful faith. What are they (note vv. 19–20, 24–26, 29–33, 39–42; see also 5:11–12)?

What is Jesus' central point in Matthew 10:34–39 (note especially v. 39)? If truly believed, how would this provide deep stability amid persecution? Consider how this attitude is reflected in Philippians 1:21 and 3:7–11.

Read through the following three sections on *Gospel Glimpses*, *Whole-Bible Connections*, and *Theological Soundings*. Then take time to consider the *Personal Implications* these sections may have for you.

## Gospel Glimpses

**INDISCRIMINATE GRACE.** The Pharisees asked Jesus' disciples, "Why does your teacher eat with tax collectors and sinners?" (Matt. 9:11). This is not so much a question as an accusation. Jesus replies, "those who are well have no need of a physician, but those who are sick. . . . I came not to call the righteous, but sinners" (vv. 12–13). Posturing themselves above those who sin differently from them, the Pharisees perceived themselves to be spiritually healthy and righteous. Like them, as long as we don't think we need a savior, we won't have one. But all who come to Jesus acknowledging their need are accepted. Those who were indiscriminate with their sin can find acceptance from the Savior who is indiscriminate with his grace.

**THE MOTIVATION OF MISSION.** In Matthew 10 Jesus sends his disciples to preach the gospel and serve the needy. Immediately before this, Matthew 9:36 shows what drove it all: "When [Jesus] saw the crowds, he had compassion for them." Jesus' compassion compelled him to send the disciples on mission. Jesus' compassionate heart still drives the church's mission today. This means at least two things for us: (1) Every Christian should be comforted by this. We are rescued because Jesus looked on us—each one of us—with genuine affection. (2) Just as compassion motivated Jesus to be on mission and equip others for it, compassion should motivate us to do the same. How can we who received his compassionate grace not be motivated to extend this grace to others?

## Whole-Bible Connections

**KINGDOM RESTORATION.** In two key summary statements Matthew links Jesus' message of the kingdom with his miracles (Matt. 4:23; 9:35). Jesus' kingdom proclamation is about the renewal of all things, and his miracles picture this very renewal. "The gospel of the kingdom" is the announcement of the removal of creation's curse. Since Genesis 3, the world has been infested with sickness, deadly storms, demonic oppression, sin, death, and disabilities. Jesus arrives and heals sickness (8:14–16), calms a deadly storm (8:23–27), ends demonic oppression (8:28–34), forgives sin (9:1–7), raises the dead (9:18–26), and heals disabilities (9:27–33). The kingdom is certainly and centrally about restoring sinners to God. But it is far more than that. It is the restoration of all things, which Jesus began at his first coming and will complete after his second.

**THE ONE WHO CALMS THE SEA.** A violent storm rages outside the boat as Jesus sleeps inside. The disciples were certainly faced with an unexpected situation, the surprising uniqueness of which only increased when Jesus "rebuked the winds and the sea" into a great calm (Matt. 8:26). "What sort of man is this," they ask, "that even winds and sea obey him?" (v. 27). According to the Old Testament, this sort of man is a divine one. God is the only one who commands the sea (Job 38:8–10; Ps. 106:9) and calms raging waters (Ps. 65:5–7; 89:8–9; 107:29). The "sort of man" this is, therefore, is "Immanuel, which means God with us" (Matt. 1:23).

## Theological Soundings

**FAITH.** Faith is more than intellectual assent to facts. It is resolute trust in a person. Three times in this section, Jesus heals on account of someone's faith (Matt. 8:13; 9:22, 29). In each case faith was not an abstract agreement with ideas but a firm confidence in the ability of Jesus to heal (read 8:8; 9:21, 28). Faith is not a magical power in itself, nor does Jesus promise to do everything we want him to do. We are not to put our faith in our faith, but in Jesus and his ability to heal and save.

**COMFORTING CONTROL.** Why shouldn't we fear those who can kill our bodies (Matt. 10:28)? Jesus answers: "Are not two sparrows sold for a penny? And not one of them will fall to the ground apart from your Father. But even the hairs of your head are all numbered" (vv. 29–30). In other words, "if birds don't fall to the ground apart from God's will, and if your hair doesn't fall to the ground apart from God's will (it's numbered!), then *you* certainly won't fall to the ground apart from God's will." Mysterious as it is, not even deadly persecution falls outside of God's control, as we see most clearly with Jesus (Acts 2:23; 4:27–28). Jesus teaches God's sovereignty[3] as a deeply comforting reality.

## Personal Implications

Take time to reflect on and make notes on the personal implications of Matthew for your own life today regarding the (1) *Gospel Glimpses*, (2) *Whole-Bible Connections*, (3) *Theological Soundings*, and (4) this passage as a whole. Also consider what you have learned that might lead you to praise God, repent of sin, trust his gracious promises, and live in obedience to him.

### 1. Gospel Glimpses

## 2. Whole-Bible Connections

## 3. Theological Soundings

## 4. Matthew 8–10

## As You Finish This Unit . . .

Take a moment now to ask for the Lord's blessing and help as you continue in this study of Matthew. And take a moment also to look back through this unit of study, to reflect on a few key things that the Lord may be teaching you—and perhaps to highlight and underline these things to review again in the future.

### Definitions

[1] **Demon** – An evil spirit that can inhabit a human being and influence him or her to carry out its will. Demons appear to be angels that fell along with Satan; they were created by God and are always limited by God. All demons will one day be destroyed along with Satan (Matt. 25:41; Rev. 20:10).

[2] **Pharisee** – A member of a popular religious/political party in NT times characterized by strict adherence to the law of Moses and also to extrabiblical Jewish traditions. The Pharisees were frequently criticized by Jesus for their legalistic, hypocritical, and self-deceived practices.

[3] **Sovereignty** – Supreme and independent power and authority. Sovereignty over all things is a distinctive attribute of God (1 Tim. 6:15–16). He directs all things to carry out his purposes (Rom. 8:28–29).

# WEEK 6: EMERGING OPPOSITION TO JESUS AND PARABLES OF THE KINGDOM

Matthew 11–13

▲

Up to this point Matthew has shown us the heart of Jesus' authoritative teaching (Matthew 5–7) as well as his authoritative ministry and mission (Matthew 8–10). Moving through chapters 11–13 we continue to see mixed responses to Jesus. As opposition more clearly emerges, Jesus begins speaking in parables in order to reveal the truth about his kingdom to some and to hide it from others. Those with "ears to hear" learn that the kingdom has arrived, but not in the way nor in the form that many expected.

## The Big Picture

Matthew 11–13 shows us the mixed responses to Jesus and his ministry and then presents Jesus' teaching on the unique nature of the kingdom of heaven.

> ## Reflection and Discussion

Read through the complete passage for this study, Matthew 11–13. Then think through and write your own notes on the following questions. (For further background, see the *ESV Study Bible*, pages 1842–1850, available online at esv.org.)

### 1. Various Responses to Jesus the Messiah (11:1–12:50)

John expected the Messiah to bring both blessing and judgment immediately. Sitting confused in prison, he wonders if Jesus really is "the one who is to come" (Matt. 11:3). Read the promises of the coming day of salvation in Isaiah 29:18–19; 35:5–6; and 61:1. What similarities do these have with Jesus' message to John in Matthew 11:4–5? What is Jesus' purpose in sending this message to him?

-------------------------------------------------------------

-------------------------------------------------------------

-------------------------------------------------------------

-------------------------------------------------------------

-------------------------------------------------------------

-------------------------------------------------------------

A "yoke" is a wooden frame joining two animals (usually oxen) for pulling loads. Jesus viewed the religious legalism of his day as an oppressive burden (see Matt. 23:4). According to Matthew 11:28–30, how does Jesus describe his character, his "yoke," and his promise for those who come to him? What does it mean to "come" to Jesus in this context?

-------------------------------------------------------------

-------------------------------------------------------------

-------------------------------------------------------------

-------------------------------------------------------------

-------------------------------------------------------------

-------------------------------------------------------------

The Pharisees accused Jesus' disciples of breaking the law by plucking grain on the Sabbath,[1] which the Pharisees viewed as a form of "work" (Matt. 12:1–2). Jesus defends these actions by providing examples from the Old Testament where certain commands or principles were formally set aside in order to obey the intention of the law or a command of a higher priority. How do we see this with the examples from David (vv. 3–4), the priests (v. 5), and the quotation from Hosea 6:6 (v. 7)? How is this also seen in the following story in Matthew 12:9–14?

------

------

------

------

------

------

The Pharisees suggest that Jesus' ability to cast out demons shows that he is in league with Satan (Matt. 12:24). How does Jesus logically turn this accusation against them? What does Jesus go on to say are the real implications of his power over demons?

------

------

------

------

------

------

As Matthew's Gospel progresses, Jesus becomes increasingly polarizing. Identify several ways we see this in Matthew 12:33–50. How does Jesus characterize the people who respond positively to him, according to 12:46–50?

------

------

------

------

------

------

## 2. The Mystery of the Kingdom Revealed (13:1–58)

Jesus tells the parable of the sower in Matthew 13:1–9 and explains it to his disciples in verses 18–23. What do the seed and soils represent, and what is the fundamental difference between the first three kinds of soil and the fourth? In what way does Jesus' explanation of the purpose of parables in verses 10–17 expand our understanding of this difference?

For those who are able to receive Jesus' message, his parables explain the unexpected nature of the kingdom of God (see Matt. 13:11). What is the central point of each of the following parables: the parable of the weeds (13:24–30; 36–43), the mustard seed (13:31–32), and the leaven (13:33)? How does each clarify the nature of the kingdom?

What do the parables of the hidden treasure (13:44) and the valuable pearl (13:45–46) teach about the kingdom? What greater clarity does this add to the call to self-denial in Matthew 10:38–39?

**Read through the following three sections on *Gospel Glimpses*, *Whole-Bible Connections*, and *Theological Soundings*. Then take time to consider the *Personal Implications* these sections may have for you.**

**FRIEND OF SINNERS.** The Pharisees are appalled when they see the people with whom Jesus spends his time. "Look at him!" they exclaim, "A glutton and a drunkard, a friend of tax collectors and sinners!" (Matt. 11:19). They wouldn't expect a moral leader to befriend the most notoriously immoral people of all. Haven't these people declared their opposition to God by their lifestyles? That Jesus would relax into the evening with them is a scandal! Yet he did. This was what he came to do, to make his enemies his friends at the cost of his own life. On his way to the cross, he told his disciples, "Greater love has no one than this, that someone lay down his life for his friends" (John 15:13).

**REST.** When Jesus looked out at the people of the world, he saw weariness. They're not worn out by physical labor but by religious work. They were burdened by the additional rules stacked high on their backs by the religious leaders (Matt. 23:4). False religion and legalism create a downward spiral of trying hard, failing, trying harder, and failing more. This leads to guilt from past failure, fear of future failure, and pride from any perceived measure of success. Jesus provides an exit from this life-sapping cycle. His answer isn't found in obeying more rules or different rules, but in himself. "Come to me, all who labor and are heavy laden, and I will give you rest . . . for I am gentle and lowly in heart" (Matt. 11:28). Jesus' fundamental orientation to the spiritually worn-out is not further critique and condemnation, but gentleness and welcome. True rest, rest from all our weary working, is found in him.

**THE TREASURE OF THE KINGDOM.** A man comes upon a treasure hidden in a field and "in his joy he goes and sells all that he has and buys that field" (Matt. 13:44). He's no fool. He's trading everything he has for something better. The kingdom of heaven is like this treasure. We may lose everything to gain it, but we come out ahead. There is no ultimate self-denial with Jesus. He doesn't lead us on a path away from joy, but directly toward it. Those who understand this gladly give up all lesser treasures for the sake of Christ (see also Phil. 3:7–8; Heb. 10:34).

**JESUS, THE TRUE AND GREATER.** We can hardly read through Matthew 12 without being struck by Jesus' radical statements about his identity in relation to the Old Testament. "I tell you, something greater than the temple is here" (12:6). "Behold, something greater than Jonah is here" (12:41). "Behold, something greater than Solomon is here" (12:42). He also implied that he was greater than King David and the priests, and he calls himself the "Lord of the

Sabbath" (12:1–7). Notice that he didn't just compare himself to all these people or institutions as being equal to them. He supersedes them. Jesus is the One to whom all these institutions and people point. He is the true and greater prophet, priest, and king. Therefore, we must listen to his prophetic word, receive his priestly ministry, and submit to his kingly rule.

**THE MYSTERY OF THE KINGDOM.** Jesus launched his ministry with the startling announcement that "the kingdom of heaven is at hand" (Matt. 4:17; see 12:28). Yet the kingdom's arrival didn't match people's expectations. Two things were expected to occur immediately and simultaneously: God would save his people and judge his enemies. But Matthew 13 tells us that the kingdom of heaven has indeed arrived in Jesus, but it will not be fully consummated until the distant future. Like a tiny mustard seed that grows into a tree, the kingdom begins small and grows into its full expression over time (13:31–32).

## Theological Soundings

**TRUE AND FALSE FAITH.** Jesus' parable of the sower shows four different responses to his message. The first one hears but doesn't understand (Matt. 13:19). The second responds joyfully but then falls away (vv. 20–21). The third endures for a while but "proves unfruitful" (v. 22). Only the fourth proves to be fruitful (v. 23). What might appear on the surface to be faith may prove to be false. Only the fourth is genuine, which is evidenced by its fruitfulness. As Jesus said, "the tree is known by its fruit" (12:33–35; see 7:15–20).

**GOD'S SOVEREIGNTY AND HUMAN RESPONSIBILITY.** On two different occasions in Matthew 11–13 Jesus teaches that God is ultimately sovereign over the ability of people to understand his revelation. The ability to spiritually "hear" the message of the kingdom is a gift that God gives only to some (Matt. 13:10–11). At the same time, he calls *all* to "hear" his message (v. 18; similarly, see 11:25–27). Throughout the Bible we see that God is sovereign over all things and humans are responsible for their actions. That both truths are present together in Scripture means that we don't have to reject one to preserve the other. God is sovereign and humans are responsible. Difficult as it is for us to hold these two together, these twin truths are ultimately compatible, not contradictory.

## Personal Implications

Take time to reflect on various implications of Matthew for your own life today. Additionally, consider what you have learned that might lead you to praise God, repent of sin, trust his gracious promises, and live in obedience to him. Make notes below on the personal implications for your walk with the Lord of the (1) *Gospel Glimpses*, (2) *Whole-Bible Connections*, (3) *Theological Soundings*, and (4) this passage as a whole.

## 1. Gospel Glimpses

## 2. Whole-Bible Connections

## 3. Theological Soundings

## 4. Matthew 11–13

## As You Finish This Unit . . .

Take a moment now to ask for the Lord's blessing and help as you continue in this study of Matthew. And take a moment also to look back through this unit of study, to reflect on a few key things that the Lord may be teaching you—and perhaps to highlight and underline these things to review again in the future.

**Definitions**

[1] **Sabbath** – Saturday, the seventh day of the week, the Jewish day of worship and rest (Gen. 2:2–3; Ex. 31:13–17).

# Week 7: Growing Clarity about the Messiah's Identity

Matthew 14–17

▲

## The Place of the Passage

As Jesus continues to speak the message of the kingdom and demonstrate its power in his actions, people respond in diverse ways. These themes continue into this section, with an added emphasis on Jesus' identity. While chapter 13 clarified the surprising nature of the kingdom of heaven, chapters 14–17 clarify the surprising identity of Jesus. Once Peter rightly identifies Jesus as "the Christ" (16:16), Jesus immediately begins to head toward Jerusalem, while teaching that he must suffer and die (16:21). From this point onward, the cross is clearly in view.

## The Big Picture

In Matthew 14–17 we gain an increasing clarity about the identity of Jesus as the Messiah who has come to suffer.

> ## Reflection and Discussion

Read through the complete passage for this study, Matthew 14–17. Then review the questions below concerning this section of Matthew's account of the gospel and write your notes on them. (For further background, see the *ESV Study Bible*, pages 1850–1858, available online at esv.org.)

### 1. Fear, Doubt, and Faith in the Messiah (14:1–16:12)

Herod hears about Jesus and thinks he is John the Baptist (Matt. 14:1–2). Matthew has already shown similarities between John and Jesus (for example, 3:2; 4:17). In light of this, how does the story about John in Matthew 14:1–12 anticipate what will happen to Jesus?

The scene of Jesus' miraculous feeding recalls the nation of Israel wandering in the wilderness after the exodus and God's gracious provision of manna (Exodus 16). The significance of 12 basketfuls may be that it recalls the 12 tribes of Israel. How do the disciples' responses to Jesus in Matthew 14:15 parallel Moses' response to God in Numbers 11:21–22?

Jesus walks on the raging sea and declares to his terrified disciples, "Take heart; it is I. Do not be afraid" (Matt. 14:27). "It is I" is *ego eimi* in Greek; literally, "I am"— a phrase that shows up first in God's naming of himself in Exodus 3:14

and subsequently in Isaiah 41:4; 43:10. Read those texts as well as Isaiah 41:10 and 43:1–10 as you consider what Jesus is here declaring about himself.

When the Pharisees indignantly asked why Jesus' disciples disregard one of their religious rules, Jesus responds by calling them hypocrites. Identify the reasons Jesus gives for calling them this (Matt. 15:1–9). According to Jesus' teaching in the following section in Matthew 15:10–20 (esp. vv. 18–20), what do the Pharisees not understand?

Nearly all of Jesus' ministry took place within the traditional borders of Israel in areas dominated by Jews. Yet Matthew 15:21–39 presents Jesus traveling in Gentile territory. What do the three stories in this section show us about the response of Gentiles to him?

## 2. The Identity of the Messiah Revealed (16:13–17:27)

How does Matthew 16:18 explain the continual existence of the church,[1] its value, and our hope for the future? How do you see the church undervalued today?

Peter said more than he knew when he confessed Jesus to be the Christ (the Messiah). Read Matthew 16:21–23 and identify what Peter missed. How does Jesus' mission clash with the widespread expectation that the coming Christ would immediately assert his kingdom with force and overthrow the rule of the Romans? How does this fill out our understanding of Jesus' call to discipleship in 16:24–26?

How might the story of Jesus' transfiguration in Matthew 17:1–8 clarify part of what Jesus meant in 16:28? Consider 2 Peter 1:16–18 with your answer.

The transfiguration account is rich with allusions to the time when Moses went up a mountain to meet with God. Read Exodus 24:12–18 closely and note any parallels you see with Matthew 17:1–8. After noting the connections, consider what this teaches about Jesus.

The disciples weren't able to cast out a demon. According to Jesus, they should have been able to do so. Indeed, they should be able to "move mountains," a metaphor for doing the seemingly impossible (see 1 Cor. 13:2). What did they lack? What does this teach us about the importance of trusting God's ability to accomplish his purposes through us?

---------------------------------------------------------------

---------------------------------------------------------------

---------------------------------------------------------------

---------------------------------------------------------------

---------------------------------------------------------------

Read through the following three sections on *Gospel Glimpses*, *Whole-Bible Connections*, and *Theological Soundings*. Then take time to consider the *Personal Implications* these sections may have for you.

## ▶ Gospel Glimpses

**WEAK FAITH, POWERFUL GOD.** "If you have faith like a grain of mustard seed," Jesus says, "nothing will be impossible for you" (Matt. 17:21). Jesus is not saying, "the more faith you have, the more you can accomplish." If he was, he might have referred to faith being like a giant mountain rather than a tiny seed. Even if our faith is *that small*, he says, we can do the seemingly impossible. Why? Because the power is not in the *amount* of our faith, but in the *object* of faith. It's not about the strength of our faith, but the strength of the One in whom we trust. The point being made isn't about the quality of our faith, but the fact that our faith is in Jesus.

**NO ULTIMATE SELF-DENIAL.** In the first century the cross was a symbol of execution. To take up one's cross was to embrace the path that leads to death. This is what Jesus calls his disciples to do (Matt. 16:24). But with Jesus, this is not ultimate self-denial. It's actually a rational exchange, for what we gain is greater than what we lose. He says, "For whoever would save his life will lose it, but whoever loses his life for my sake will find it" (16:25). As the missionary Jim Elliot put it, "He is no fool who gives what he cannot keep to gain that which he cannot lose."

## ▶ Whole-Bible Connections

**THE SHEPHERD-KING.** In both of Jesus' miraculous feedings, he heals people (Matt. 14:14; 15:30–31), has "compassion" on them (14:14; 15:32), and

55

feeds them abundantly (14:20; 15:37). Note also that people "sit down on the grass" in the first (14:19) and are on a "mountain" in the second (15:29). Such details are not insignificant. One of the great promises of salvation in the Old Testament was cast in the metaphor of God as a shepherd who would come to care for his sheep. He would heal their injuries, have them recline on the grass, and feed them abundantly on mountains (Ezek. 34:11–16). Further, it is not just God himself who would come as a shepherd; he would appoint a chief shepherd-king, David, who "shall feed them and be their shepherd" (34:23–24; 37:24). Through his miraculous feedings Jesus demonstrates that he is the long-awaited divine shepherd as well as the appointed Davidic shepherd-king. We trust him as our compassionate rescuer, healer, and provider.

**PROPHET LIKE MOSES.** When Jesus is transfigured on the mountain, the Father repeats what he spoke to him at his baptism (compare Matt. 3:17 and 17:5). Calling him his "beloved Son," the Father reaffirms Jesus as the long-awaited Davidic King (note 2 Sam. 7:12–14; Ps. 2:7–12). Calling him the one "with whom I am well pleased," he reaffirms Jesus' identity as Isaiah's promised Servant (note Isa. 42:1). But now another phrase is added: "listen to him" (Matt. 17:5). This recalls Moses' promise that "the Lord your God will raise up for you a prophet like me from among you, from your brothers—it is to him you shall listen" (Deut. 18:15). As Moses stands with Jesus at his transfiguration, he hears the Father declare Jesus to be this greatly anticipated prophet. Peter, who was also standing with them, later announces to Israel's leaders that Jesus is, indeed, the prophet like Moses (Acts 3:22–23). We must listen to and obey all that he says.

## ▶ Theological Soundings

**THE CHURCH.** In response to Peter's confession Jesus declares, "I will build my church, and the gates of hell shall not prevail against it" (Matt. 16:18). Sometimes "the church" refers to all the Christians in a particular local area who gather together and share life with one anther. We call this the "local church." Other times it refers to all of God's people across the world viewed collectively, the "universal church," which is what Jesus has in view here. The force of Jesus' declaration is that the church's continued existence and advancement in the world will not be left up to chance. He will see to the continued growth of the church because it is precious to him. He gave his blood for her (Acts 20:28; Eph. 5:25). "The gates of hell" may picture Satanic attacks on the church or Satanic resistance to the church's advance, but in either case the point is the same: in coming conflicts, the church will be victorious.

**RADICAL DEPRAVITY.** Jesus says, "Out of the heart come evil thoughts, murder, adultery, sexual immorality, theft, false witness, slander" (Matt. 15:19).

Throughout the Bible, the heart is the "control center" of our lives, the place of our deepest thoughts and desires. Jesus teaches that our problem lies far deeper than our actions, for our actions show what's really inside us. We are like a spring that always produces muddy water. In other words, we are radically depraved. That is, while we are not as bad as we could possibly be, every part of us is affected by sin, and so less good than it should be. Thankfully, Jesus didn't come to bring us a new set of religious practices to observe; he came to give us new hearts, that can begin to battle sin effectively

## ► Personal Implications

Take time to consider various implications of Matthew for your own life today. Additionally, reflect on what you have learned that might lead you to praise God, repent of sin, trust his gracious promises, and live in obedience to him. Make notes below on the personal implications for your walk with the Lord of the (1) *Gospel Glimpses*, (2) *Whole-Bible Connections*, (3) *Theological Soundings*, and (4) this passage as a whole.

### 1. Gospel Glimpses

### 2. Whole-Bible Connections

## 3. Theological Soundings

## 4. Matthew 14–17

> ## As You Finish This Unit . . .

Take a moment now to ask for the Lord's blessing and help as you continue in this study of Matthew. And take a moment also to look back through this unit of study, to reflect on a few key things that the Lord may be teaching you—and perhaps to highlight and underline these things to review again in the future.

### Definitions

[1] **Church** – From a Greek work meaning "assembly." The body of believers in Jesus Christ, referring either to a local gathering of believers or to all believers everywhere.

# WEEK 8: THE COMMUNITY OF THE KINGDOM

Matthew 18–20

## The Place of the Passage

Through the course of his ministry, Jesus has been creating a community of followers who repent in response to his teaching (Matt. 4:17) and who come to him for rest (11:28–30). These, he says, are his true family (12:49–50). As Jesus heads toward Jerusalem with this new community, he teaches them about what their life together must look like. How should they respond to sin? How will they view marriage, money, and possessions? What will it look like to be a community where the greatest are the servants? Matthew 18–20 helps us answer such questions.

## The Big Picture

In Matthew 18–20 Jesus teaches on several topics related to the radical kind of lifestyle in which he calls his new community to live together.

> **Reflection and Discussion**

Read through the complete passage for this study, Matthew 18–20. Then think through and write your own notes on the following questions. (For further background, see the *ESV Study Bible*, pages 1858–1864, available online at esv.org.)

### 1. Life Together in the New Community (18:1–35)

In Matthew 18:1–4 Jesus begins instructing his disciples about the culture of their new community by redefining greatness as humility. What does this passage teach us about humility? How does this contrast with the way that the world views greatness?

Since Matthew 18:3 states that disciples must be humble like children, it is likely that the "little ones" mentioned in verses 5–6 (and perhaps also vv. 10–14) are all true disciples (see also 10:40–42). According to these verses, how does Jesus want his people to treat every other believer?

Matthew 18:7–9 tells us what to do about our own sins[1], and 18:15–22 tells us what to do about the sins that other professing Christians commit against us. For each situation, identify (1) what we are commanded to do, and (2) the goal in addressing sin. In what sense are these loving commands and goals?

What is the main point of the story in Matthew 18:23–35? How is a bitter and unforgiving disposition wholly inconsistent with how God treats us through the cross?

## 2. Marriage and Money in the New Community (19:1–30)

When the Pharisees ask Jesus, "Is it lawful to divorce one's wife for any cause?" Jesus responds by pointing them back to God's original intent for marriage in Genesis 2:24. Note everything you learn about Jesus' teaching on marriage and divorce in Matthew 19:4–6 and verse 9, then try to bring all of this together in a one-sentence definition of marriage.

A rich man asks Jesus what he must do to have eternal life. Notice that Jesus' response includes only commands five through nine of the Ten Commandments, which are the others-oriented commands (Matt. 19:18–19; see 22:39). Jesus omitted the vertical, Godward commands, the first of which is against idolatry: "You shall have no other gods before me" (Ex. 20:3). He also omitted the tenth command about covetousness, which is elsewhere identified as idolatry, that is, valuing something above God (Ex. 20:17; Eph. 5:5; Col. 3:5). How does this help us understand what Jesus is asking the man to do in Matthew 19:21 and why the man responds with sorrow in verse 22?

61

In Matthew 19:23 Jesus says it is difficult for a rich person to enter the kingdom. Why is this so? How does this context help us understand what Jesus means in verse 26?

------

------

------

------

------

------

## 3. True Greatness in the New Community (20:1–34)

Review the story of Matthew 20:1–16. Why do the first-hired laborers grumble against the master, and how does the master respond? How is the mind-set of the first-hired laborers a potential danger for long-term faithful Christians?

------

------

------

------

------

------

Note how Jesus reverses the world's instincts about leadership and greatness in Matthew 20:25–27 (compare Matt. 18:1–4). How would you summarize the two different mind-sets? What is one area or example in your own life where your natural instincts about leadership need to be replaced by Jesus' lowly but truly great way?

------

------

------

------

------

------

------

Matthew brackets Jesus' teaching on greatness with statements about his impending death (Matt. 20:17–19, 28). Read these verses again and consider how Jesus is the clearest example of true greatness. What, then, does the cross teach us about true greatness and, more broadly, about leadership in general?

_____

_____

_____

_____

_____

_____

_____

Read through the following three sections on *Gospel Glimpses*, *Whole-Bible Connections*, and *Theological Soundings*. Then take time to consider the *Personal Implications* these sections may have for you.

## ▶ Gospel Glimpses

**WE FORGIVE BECAUSE HE FIRST FORGAVE US.** There is no mistaking Jesus' radical call to forgive[2] others. We must forgive not seven but 77 times, and always from the heart (Matt. 18:22, 35). In other words, there's really no limit. Where will we get the motivation to fuel this heart-level, boundless forgiveness? Jesus implies the answer with a story about a servant who was forgiven of an unfathomable debt, but who went on to demand repayment of a relatively minor sum. The point is that an unforgiving heart toward others is inconceivable for those who have truly been forgiven by God. When we see the kindhearted love of our Savior as the full weight of our sins are poured out on him at the cross, how can we then turn around and bitterly refuse to forgive someone else? The forgiveness of God, when truly grasped, transforms us to show this same forgiving grace to others (see Eph. 4:32; Col. 3:13).

**THE IMPOSSIBLE MADE POSSIBLE.** Jesus' conversation with the rich young man shows that entrance into the kingdom requires a radical denial of all idols in one's life, including the love of money and possessions. That the man walks away sad is evidence that he will not release his grip on greed in order to cling to Christ. This is why Jesus declares that it is difficult, indeed impossible, for the rich to enter his kingdom. Hope is not lost, however, for Jesus answers, "With man this is impossible, but with God all things are possible" (Matt. 19:26). In context, "all things" includes things like rich people entering the kingdom. In other words, God can do for us what we cannot do for ourselves, namely, give us a new heart to trust and treasure Jesus above money and possessions.

63

## ▶ Whole-Bible Connections

**MARRIAGE.** In response to the Pharisees' question about marriage and divorce, Jesus orients the discussion toward how things were "from the beginning" in Eden (Matt. 19:4, 8). A marriage is a God-given union between one man and one woman, intended for life and never to be broken through divorce (Matt. 19:4–6). Viewing the original intention of marriage "from the beginning" helps us understand it in two ways. First, Jesus shows that Moses' later teaching on divorce was not a statement of the ideal; rather, permission for divorce was granted in light of the hardness of the human heart (vv. 7–9). Second, this original intention of a faithful marriage union was created to picture another marriage, that of Jesus and the church (Eph. 5:25–32; Rev. 21:2–3).

**THE NEW WORLD.** Throughout Jesus' conversation with the rich young man several terms are used as near synonyms. The man asks what he must do to "have eternal life" (Matt. 19:16). Jesus speaks of entering "life" (v. 17), entering the "kingdom of heaven" (v. 23), being part of the coming "new world" (v. 28; literally, "the regeneration," or renewal of all things), and inheriting "eternal life" (v. 29). The disciples interpret all of this in terms of being "saved" (v. 25). The great hope of salvation held out in the Bible is robust enough to be referred to by a number of terms. Central to this hope is reconciliation with God through the forgiveness of sins, but our ultimate salvation includes participating in the future renewal of the world. Christians will be raised from the dead to live a flourishing bodily life with God in a new creation forever (see 1 Cor. 15:20–26; Phil. 3:20–21; Rev. 19:7; 21:1–5).

## ▶ Theological Soundings

**CHURCH DISCIPLINE.** In 18:15–20 Jesus outlines a process for responding to one disciple who sins against another. Christians refer to this as "church discipline." This text can guide our process of loving correction in several ways: First, we must address sin in the lives of Christian brothers and sisters: "If your brother sins against you, go and tell him his fault" (v. 15). Second, sins are first to be dealt with personally and privately. Only if there is a refusal to repent should the process progress to a conversation with two others, and then, if necessary, with the whole believing community (vv. 15–17). Finally, the motivation throughout must be love, and the goal is restoration: "If he listens to you, you have gained your brother" (v. 15; see vv. 12–14; compare 1 Cor. 5:5). This text assumes that local churches will be marked by this kind of courageous and loving discipline.

**ATONEMENT.** Jesus tells his disciples why he is headed to Jerusalem: "The Son of Man came not to be served but to serve, and to give his life as a ransom for many" (Matt. 20:28). A ransom refers to a payment offered in exchange for the release of another person. Jesus offers his own life as a payment in exchange for the release of others. At the heart of the gospel is the selfless love of Jesus who gave himself as a payment in exchange for our release. This is often referred to as *penal substitutionary atonement*. Jesus paid the penalty that our sins deserve (penal) by giving up his own life in our place (substitution) so that we might be restored to God (atonement).

## ▶ Personal Implications

Take time to reflect on various implications of Matthew for your own life today. Additionally, consider what you have learned that might lead you to praise God, repent of sin, trust his gracious promises, and live in obedience to him. Make notes below on the personal implications for your walk with the Lord regarding the (1) *Gospel Glimpses*, (2) *Whole-Bible Connections*, (3) *Theological Soundings*, and (4) this passage as a whole.

### 1. Gospel Glimpses

### 2. Whole-Bible Connections

### 3. Theological Soundings

## 4. Matthew 18–20

---

### As You Finish This Unit . . .

Take a moment now to ask for the Lord's blessing and help as you continue in this study of Matthew. And take a moment also to look back through this unit of study, to reflect on a few key things that the Lord may be teaching you—and perhaps to highlight and underline these things to review again in the future.

### Definitions

[1] **Sin** – A violation of or failure to adhere to the commands of God, or the desire to do so.

[2] **Forgiveness** – Release from guilt and the reestablishment of a peaceful relationship. Forgiveness can be granted by God to human beings (Luke 24:47; 1 John 1:9) and by human beings to those who have wronged them (Matt. 18:21–22; Col. 3:13).

# WEEK 9: JERUSALEM CONDEMNED FOR REJECTING THE MESSIAH

Matthew 21–23

▲

Matthew 16:21 was a turning point in Jesus' ministry, for "from that time Jesus began to show his disciples that he must go to Jerusalem and suffer many things . . . and be killed, and on the third day be raised." The focus in Matthew 21–23 is on the religious leaders' opposition to Jesus as he arrives in Jerusalem. Jesus responds by rebuking them in the form of parables (21:28–22:14), debating with them (22:15–45), and pronouncing woes upon them (23:1–39). This prepares us for the coming chapters when the conflict will climax in the crucifixion of Jesus.

## The Big Picture

In Matthew 21–23 Jesus arrives in Jerusalem amid praise but soon engages in conflict with the Jewish leaders about his own identity and their rejection of him.

## Reflection and Discussion

Read through the complete passage for this study, Matthew 21–23. Then review the questions below concerning this section of Matthew's Gospel and write your notes on them. (For further background, see the *ESV Study Bible*, pages 1864–1872, available online at esv.org.)

### 1. Jesus Confronts Jerusalem for Its Rejection of Him (21:1–22:45)

Read Zechariah 9:9–10 and consider the significance of Jesus' actions in Matthew 21:2–7. Next, read Psalm 118:25–26 in the context of the whole Psalm to discern what the crowds mean by quoting this psalm in Matthew 21:9 (note that *Hosanna* is a Greek transliteration of the Hebrew word *hoshi'ah na'*, which means "save us, we pray!"; Ps. 118:25). Bring these observations together by stating what this scene communicates about Jesus' identity.

-------------------------------------------------------------------

-------------------------------------------------------------------

-------------------------------------------------------------------

-------------------------------------------------------------------

-------------------------------------------------------------------

-------------------------------------------------------------------

Jesus curses the tree in Matthew 21:18–27 because it has only the appearance of fruit. This is an enacted parable for the events occurring this week in Jerusalem. Scan the context of Matthew 21–23 and answer these questions: What does the fig tree represent? What does Jesus' judgment against it represent?

-------------------------------------------------------------------

-------------------------------------------------------------------

-------------------------------------------------------------------

-------------------------------------------------------------------

-------------------------------------------------------------------

When the leaders confront Jesus in the temple, he exposes their ignorance and false motives. Then he proceeds to tell three parabolic stories, each of which is a retelling of the story of Israel up to the current generation. What is Jesus' central message to these leaders in . . .

. . . the story of the two sons (21:28–32)?

--------------------------------------------------------------------------

--------------------------------------------------------------------------

--------------------------------------------------------------------------

--------------------------------------------------------------------------

--------------------------------------------------------------------------

. . . the story of the tenants (21:33–46)?

--------------------------------------------------------------------------

--------------------------------------------------------------------------

--------------------------------------------------------------------------

--------------------------------------------------------------------------

. . . the story of the wedding feast (22:1–14)?

--------------------------------------------------------------------------

--------------------------------------------------------------------------

--------------------------------------------------------------------------

--------------------------------------------------------------------------

In response to Jesus' parables, the leaders "plotted how to entangle him in his words" (Matt. 22:15). They do this by asking a series of three questions. What is Jesus' primary point in his response to the Pharisees' first question (vv. 16–22)? As you consider your answer, note two things: The "image" on the coins was of the emperor, Caesar, and all humans are made in the "image" of God (Gen. 1:26–27; 9:6).

--------------------------------------------------------------------------

--------------------------------------------------------------------------

--------------------------------------------------------------------------

--------------------------------------------------------------------------

--------------------------------------------------------------------------

--------------------------------------------------------------------------

The theme of a future, bodily resurrection of the dead is developed through-out the Old Testament but is not as explicit in the Pentateuch[1] (see Isa. 26:19; Ezekiel 37; Dan. 12:2). The Sadducees did not believe in the resurrection since they drew mainly or exclusively on the Pentateuch for doctrine. In response to their questions, Jesus accuses them of knowing "neither the Scriptures nor the power of God" (Matt. 22:29). How does Jesus substantiate this claim?

Read 2 Samuel 7:12–14; Psalm 89:3–4; Isaiah 11:1–5, 10; and Jeremiah 23:5–6. With these texts in mind, is the Pharisees' response to Jesus in Matthew 22:42 correct, incorrect, or incomplete? Why does David call his descendant "my Lord," in the text Jesus quotes (Ps. 110:1)?

## 2. Jesus Condemns Jerusalem for Its Rejection of Him (23:1–39)

What does Jesus repeatedly call the leaders in Matthew 23? How do verses 1–7 demonstrate this to be an accurate name? How does this problem show up in our own lives today?

Summarize several of the prominent issues Jesus addresses in his seven "woes" to the leaders in Matthew 23:13–36. Can you identify places earlier in Matthew where this teaching also occurs?

How does Jesus' climactic lament over Jerusalem in Matthew 23:37–39 inform us about how Jesus thinks and feels about those who reject him?

Read through the following three sections on *Gospel Glimpses*, *Whole-Bible Connections*, and *Theological Soundings*. Then take time to consider the *Personal Implications* these sections may have for you.

## Gospel Glimpses

**UNWORTHY WORTHINESS.** Jesus compares his kingdom to a wedding feast that a king throws for his son. Those invited first refuse to come and are therefore pronounced "not worthy" (Matt. 22:8). The king then sends his invitation to the streets and many come to the feast, "both bad and good" (v. 10). Apparently unworthiness is not about being bad, for those who finally come to the feast are "both bad and good." Likewise, worthiness is not about being good, for the first invitees are judged unworthy simply because they refused the invitation. Worthiness here is not based on moral performance but on a willingness to come to the king's party. In other words, worthiness is about a willingness to receive grace. The kingdom's entrance invitation does not say, "are you good enough?" but, "whether 'good' or 'bad', are you willing to come?"

71

**INTENTIONAL SACRIFICE.** The leaders question Jesus' authority (Matt. 21:23), wish to arrest him (21:46), and seek to trap him in his words (22:15). He will be murdered in only a few short days. How do we explain why Jesus stays here amid such persecution? Matthew has already shown the answer. This is the outworking of Jesus' own plan, for he told his disciples earlier that "he *must* go to Jerusalem and suffer many things from the elders and chief priests and scribes, and be killed, and on the third day be raised" (16:21; see also 17:22–23; 20:17–19). Jesus willingly endured this opposition, suffering, and ultimately crucifixion for us, for he was giving his life as our ransom[2] (20:28).

## ▶ Whole-Bible Connections

**THE STORY OF ISRAEL AND THE REJECTION OF JESUS.** In Matthew 21:33–46 Jesus told a story of a master farmer who planted a vineyard and leased it to tenants. When the master sent servants to the tenants to gather fruit, the tenants beat, killed, and stoned them. When the master sent his own son, they killed him as well. This is Israel's story, for they were often referred to as a vineyard in the Old Testament (Isa. 5:1–7; Ps. 80:8–11). The master, then, is God, and the tenants were Israel's leaders. By climaxing the story with the rejection of the master's son and the subsequent judgment on the tenants, Jesus declares that the events of his ministry are the climax of the story of Israel. The leaders of Israel have rejected God's prophets for hundreds of years and are now about to murder his own Son.

**THE REJECTED STONE.** Words from Psalm 118 are woven throughout these chapters. The Psalm describes a divine rescue of one who appears to be a king (vv. 5–18), followed by his procession to Jerusalem, and then the temple where the people celebrate his victory, saying, "the stone that the builders rejected has become the cornerstone" (v. 22). Just like a rejected stone that becomes the most important one, this rejected king is now victorious. They rejoice in his arrival with the words, "Blessed is he who comes in the name of the LORD" (vv. 25–26). Yet they also cry out for further deliverance: "save us, we pray" (Greek, *hosanna*). This request is finally being answered in Jesus. Just like the king in Psalm 118, Jesus enters Jerusalem and the temple with crowds shouting, "Hosanna to the Son of David! Blessed is he who comes in the name of the Lord" (Matt. 21:9; see v. 15). Jesus also quotes Psalm 118:22 to the leaders who are rejecting him. Just as the "builders" rejected the "stone" in Psalm 118, these leaders will reject Jesus (Matt. 21:42–44). But, as the apostle Peter later told these very leaders after the resurrection, "This Jesus is the stone that was rejected by you, the builders, which has become the cornerstone" (Acts 4:8–11).

## Theological Soundings

**RESURRECTION.** In response to a question from the Sadducees about the nature of life and marriage after the resurrection, Jesus says, "In the resurrection they neither marry nor are given in marriage, but are like angels in heaven" (Matt. 22:30). The life God's people will live when they're raised from the dead will have similarities to and differences from the life they live now (see 1 Cor. 15:35–58; Phil. 3:20–21). We will be similar to angels in that we will not be in marriage relationships (perhaps because we will have reached that to which marriages pointed all along, the marital union between Christ and the church). Yet we will also be different from angels, for we will continue to live as humans in resurrected, physical bodies.

**DIVINITY OF JESUS.** The children praise Jesus and cry out, "Hosanna to the Son of David!" (Matt. 21:15). When the leaders become indignant upon hearing this, Jesus defends the children's actions by referencing Psalm 8:2: "Out of the mouth of infants and nursing babies you have prepared praise" (Matt. 21:16). Those familiar with Psalm 8 would recognize that it was referring to the praise of *God*. Here we see Jesus' implicit teaching of his own divinity. Any praise offered to Jesus is rightly understood as praise to God.

## Personal Implications

Take time to think about and make notes on the personal implications of Matthew for your own life today regarding the (1) *Gospel Glimpses*, (2) *Whole-Bible Connections*, (3) *Theological Soundings*, and (4) this passage as a whole. Also consider what you have learned that might lead you to praise God, repent of sin, trust his gracious promises, and live in obedience to him.

### 1. Gospel Glimpses

### 2. Whole-Bible Connections

## 3. Theological Soundings

## 4. Matthew 21–23

> ## As You Finish This Unit . . .

Take a moment now to ask for the Lord's blessing and help as you continue in this study of Matthew. And take a moment also to look back through this unit of study, to reflect on a few key things that the Lord may be teaching you—and perhaps to highlight and underline these things to review again in the future.

### Definitions

[1] **Pentateuch** – The first five books of the Bible.

[2] **Ransom** – A price paid to redeem, or buy back, someone who has become enslaved or something that has been lost to someone else.

# Week 10: Jerusalem's Impending Judgment and Anticipating the End

Matthew 24–25

▲

The conflict of Matthew 21–23 leads to Jesus pronouncing "woes" upon the religious leaders. Now he announces a coming judgment against the temple and various trials that will characterize the age until his future return. This leads to a series of parables that Jesus gives to encourage his people to be prepared for his return. Although the following chapters will show Jesus' death and resurrection, we already learn that he will be leaving, after those events, for an indefinite period of time.

## The Big Picture

In Matthew 24–25 Jesus announces judgment against Jerusalem, teaches about the coming trials, and motivates his followers to prepare for his glorious return.

## Reflection and Discussion

Read through the complete passage for this study, Matthew 24–25. Then think through and write your own notes on the following questions. (For further background, see the *ESV Study Bible*, pages 1873–1879, available online at esv.org.)

### 1. The Trials of This Age, the Judgment of Jerusalem, and the Return of Jesus (24:1–35)

As they walk alongside the Mount of Olives, the disciples point to the beautiful temple[1] in the distance. How does Jesus respond and how did the end of Matthew 23 prepare us for this statement (note that their temple was often referred to as a "house")?

Matthew 24:4–35 is Jesus' answer to his disciples' questions, "when will these things be?" (that is, the judgment of the temple and Jerusalem), and "what will be the sign of your coming and of the end of the age?" (v. 3). Jesus first gives a general description of what the disciples should expect to be normal characteristics of their lifetime and beyond (24:4–14). What are they to expect? According to verses 4–6, why did Jesus tell his disciples about these impending trials (see also vv. 22–28)? What lessons should we learn from this?

In Matthew 24:15–21 Jesus fills out what he meant when he spoke of the Jews' "house" being left desolate, that is, their temple being destroyed (23:38; 24:2). According to historical records, the fall of Jerusalem to the Romans in AD 70 was indeed a horrible devastation. Identify the specific ways that Jesus assumes his disciples might be deceived (24:22–28). What does Jesus say in order to keep them from being deceived?

It is difficult to discern what Matthew 24:34 means. Some understand "this generation" as referring to the people alive at the time while "all these things" refers to the beginning but not the completion of the events described in verses 4–28. However we understand the details, how does verse 35 give us confidence in the ultimate fulfillment of such things?

## 2. Preparing for the Return of Jesus (24:36–25:46)

Jesus compares his return to the sudden judgment of the flood in Noah's day, where some people were judged and the others saved (Matt. 24:37–41). What is Jesus' central point about the nature of his return? What does "stay awake" (v. 42) mean, and how do 1 Thessalonians 5:1–8; 1 Peter 4:7; and 2 Peter 3:10–13 fill out our understanding of how we are to live in light of Christ's second coming?

Five parables in Matthew 24:42–25:46 each uniquely fill out the theme of preparedness for Jesus' return. What is the point of the first parable (24:42–44)?

Note the behavior and destiny of the "wicked servant" in the second parable, Matthew 24:45–51. What does this indicate about whether or not he is a true disciple (consult 1 Cor. 6:9–11 and Gal. 5:19–21)?

As the parable of the ten virgins indicates, Jesus' return will be after a lengthy period of time (Matt. 25:5; see also 24:48; 25:19). Identify the main lesson for God's people regarding this period of waiting. What do we learn about the importance of heeding this lesson when we compare Jesus' response in 25:12 with his similar response in 7:21–23?

Review the fourth parable of Matthew 25:14–30 and note the identical praise given to the first two servants even though both earned different amounts. What does this indicate about what is most important to the master? How, then, does Jesus want us to live in light of his return?

What is the fundamental difference between the sheep and the goats at the last judgment? (vv. 32–33). Additionally, who are the hungry, sick, needy, or imprisoned "least of these my brothers" of Jesus? (v. 40). Consider your answer in light of other texts in Matthew where we read of the identity of Jesus' "brothers" (Matt. 12:48–50; 23:8; 28:10) and those he calls "little ones" (10:42; 18:6, 14), as well as his statements about his missionary disciples in 10:40–42.

Read through the following three sections on *Gospel Glimpses*, *Whole-Bible Connections*, and *Theological Soundings*. Then take time to consider the *Personal Implications* these sections may have for you.

## Gospel Glimpses

**COMMENDED FAITHFULNESS.** When the servants invest and multiply the money their master gave them, the master responds, "Well done, good and faithful servant" (Matt. 25:21, 23). This is a picture of the gracious and generous commendation Jesus will give all of his servants when he returns. The apostle Paul likewise affirms that, "each one will receive his commendation from God" (1 Cor. 4:5; see Rom. 2:29; Heb. 11:2, 4, 5, 39). This is over-the-top generosity to sinners. All of our works are done in response to and empowered by God and his grace (Rom. 2:26–29; Gal. 5:22; Phil. 2:13). Moreover, they are also imperfect and require the sacrifice of Jesus for them to be acceptable. Yet God will commend his people for the very things he has enabled them to do! This is why his praise of us will ultimately redound not to our glory but to his.

**THE GIFT OF THE KINGDOM.** At the final judgment, Jesus will say, "Come, you who are blessed by my Father, inherit the kingdom prepared for you from the foundation of the world" (Matt. 25:34). An "inheritance" isn't worked for or earned; it is received. While Jesus points to the selfless service of those who will ultimately be saved, the ultimate reason for their entrance into his kingdom is grace. It's a gift. The sheep's surprise at hearing of their own works demonstrates that none of these works were done for the sake of repayment

(25:37–39). With Jesus, earning is out of the question. He gives his kingdom on terms of grace.

## Whole-Bible Connections

**ABOMINATION OF DESOLATION.** Jesus warns about "the abomination of desolation spoken of by the prophet Daniel" (Matt. 24:15). Daniel 11:31 speaks of those who will profane Israel's temple and fortress and "shall set up the abomination that makes desolate" (see also Dan. 9:27; 12:11). This was first fulfilled in 167 BC when Antiochus Epiphanes entered the temple to set up in it an altar or idol devoted to the Greek god Zeus. Yet that was not the only time an "abomination of desolation" would appear, for Jesus clarifies that another fulfillment would happen in the Roman destruction of the temple in AD 70.

**THE SON OF MAN.** Throughout Matthew 24–25 Jesus repeatedly refers to himself as "the Son of Man" (24:27, 30, 37, 39, 44; 25:31). This title comes from a vision of the prophet Daniel: "behold, with the clouds of heaven there came one like a son of man, and he came to the Ancient of Days and was presented before him. And to him was given dominion and glory and a kingdom, that all peoples, nations, and languages should serve him" (Dan. 7:13–14). Jesus draws on the language of this text when he says, "When the Son of Man comes in his glory, and all the angels with him, then he will sit on his glorious throne" (Matt. 25:31; also 24:30). According to Matthew 28:18–20, Jesus received this authority and has begun to gather people from "all peoples, nations, and languages" to serve him. One day he will return again to rule his redeemed, multiethnic people forever.

## Theological Soundings

**ESCHATOLOGY.** Theologians use the word "eschatology" to refer to the study of the "last things" or "end times." According to the New Testament, the "end times" began when Jesus arrived on the scene to start his ministry and so begin the fulfillment of Old Testament hopes and promises. Yet Matthew 24–25 points us forward to the time of their complete fulfillment. We still await the glorious second coming of Jesus (24:36), the gathering of all believers to be with him (24:31), the final judgment (25:31–46), and the separation of all people for either eternal punishment or eternal life (25:34, 41, 46).

**JUDGMENT ACCORDING TO WORKS.** Jesus will judge all people, granting eternal life to some and sending others away to eternal punishment (Matt. 25:34, 41, 46). The reason Jesus provides for why one receives one destiny and not the other concerns a person's works (25:35–36, 42–43; see also Rom. 2:6–

11; 14:10–12; 2 Cor. 5:10; Rev. 20:11–14). Jesus isn't teaching that the *basis* of our acceptance before God is our own good works, for he immediately reminds his disciples that he will be crucified, pouring out his blood for the forgiveness of our sins (26:1, 28). While our acceptance before God is based on the forgiveness of our sins through faith in Christ alone, our good works will nevertheless provide demonstrative evidence of whether our faith is real.

## ▶ Personal Implications

Take time to reflect on various implications of Matthew for your own life today. Additionally, consider what you have learned that might lead you to praise God, repent of sin, trust his gracious promises, and live in obedience to him. Make notes below on the personal implications for your walk with the Lord regarding the (1) *Gospel Glimpses*, (2) *Whole-Bible Connections*, (3) *Theological Soundings*, and (4) this passage as a whole.

### 1. Gospel Glimpses

### 2. Whole-Bible Connections

### 3. Theological Soundings

## 4. Matthew 24–25

--------------------------------------------------------------

--------------------------------------------------------------

--------------------------------------------------------------

--------------------------------------------------------------

--------------------------------------------------------------

--------------------------------------------------------------

### As You Finish This Unit . . .

Take a moment now to ask for the Lord's blessing and help as you continue in this study of Matthew. And take a moment also to look back through this unit of study, to reflect on a few key things that the Lord may be teaching you—and perhaps to highlight and underline these things to review again in the future.

### Definitions

[1] **Temple** – A place set aside as holy because of God's presence there. Solomon built the first temple of the Lord in Jerusalem, to replace the portable tabernacle. This temple was later destroyed by the Babylonians, rebuilt after the return from exile, and destroyed again by the Romans.

# WEEK 11: THE CRUCIFIXION, RESURRECTION, AND COMMISSION OF JESUS

Matthew 26–28

> ## The Place of the Passage

We now come to the events toward which Matthew's narrative has been steadily heading from the start. Leading up to Jesus' death, we read what the political and religious leaders do: they arrest, try, convict, flog, and crucify Jesus. We read about what his disciples do: Judas betrays him, Peter denies him, and all abandon him. We also learn what Jesus does: he predicts his death, explains its meaning, and willingly endures it. And then he defeats it. The end of Matthew's gospel looks to the future, with the disciples' commission to take the gospel to all nations.

## The Big Picture

In Matthew 26–28 Jesus is condemned and crucified, and then he rises from the grave and sends his disciples on mission to the world.

## Reflection and Discussion

Read through the complete passage for this study, Matthew 26–28. Then review the questions below concerning this section of Matthew's account of the gospel and write your notes on them. (For further background, see the *ESV Study Bible*, pages 1880–1888, available online at esv.org.)

### 1. Jesus Prepares for Death (26:1–56)

Jesus predicts his death for the fourth time in the opening verses of Matthew 26 (for the first three, see Matt. 16:21; 17:22–23; and 20:17–19). Scan Matthew 26:1–56 and note other occasions where we read of Jesus' foreknowledge of coming events.

Jesus' last meal with his disciples is a Passover[1] meal, which he uses to explain the meaning of his death (Matt. 26:17–29). Review Exodus 12, where this meal was first instituted, and reflect on the significance of the Passover for understanding why Jesus died.

A cloud of deep sadness looms over Jesus' final night not only because he will soon be arrested by his enemies, but also because of the failures of his own friends. What do we learn about the weakness or sinfulness of humans from Judas's betrayal (26:14–25), the abandonment of Jesus by his disciples (26:31–35), and the weariness of his closest friends in the garden (26:36–46)?

What words are most appropriate to describe what Jesus is experiencing in the garden of Gethsemane? The reason for Jesus' current state is the prospect of a "cup" that he must drink (Matt. 26:39, 42). How do Psalm 75:7–8; Isaiah 51:17–23; Jeremiah 25:15–16; and Ezekiel 23:31–34 shed light on what this cup represents?

## 2. The Condemnation of Jesus to Death (26:57–27:56)

Among other themes woven into the account of Jesus' trial are his innocence (Matt. 26:59–60; 27:4, 19, 23) and silence (Matt. 26:62–63; 27:12–14), both of which allude back to the prophecy of Isaiah 53. Read Isaiah's prophecy and note how it is being fulfilled in these events.

The account of Jesus' crucifixion is filled with irony. The mocking soldiers often speak and act better than they know. Where do you see examples of this throughout Matthew 27:27–44?

What does Matthew 27:46 indicate about an even deeper and more profound suffering than the physical pain of the crucifixion²? What is the significance of this (think back to Matt. 1:21; 20:28; 26:26–29; and 26:39; see also Rom. 3:21–26)?

--------------------------------------------------------

--------------------------------------------------------

--------------------------------------------------------

--------------------------------------------------------

Matthew draws attention to the Gentile who is the first to confess Jesus as the "Son of God" (Matt. 27:54) and the presence of women as witnesses of Jesus' death and resurrection (27:55–56; 28:1–10). What is the significance of this emphasis? How does this connect back to passages we've seen throughout this book?

--------------------------------------------------------

--------------------------------------------------------

--------------------------------------------------------

--------------------------------------------------------

--------------------------------------------------------

### 3. The Resurrection and Commission of Jesus (27:57–28:20)

What do we see in Matthew 27:57–28:15 that emphasizes the historical reality of Jesus' death, burial, and resurrection? According to 1 Corinthians 15:12–28, why is it so important that the resurrection actually happened?

--------------------------------------------------------

--------------------------------------------------------

--------------------------------------------------------

--------------------------------------------------------

Matthew 28:16–20 culminates numerous themes in Matthew's gospel account. Identify several of these, noting their significance in Matthew and how this final scene further develops or properly climaxes each one.

--------------------------------------------------------

--------------------------------------------------------

--------------------------------------------------------

--------------------------------------------------------

Jesus' parting command is for his people to make disciples of all nations. Very practically, what does it look like to fulfill this commission? How does Jesus' kingly authority (28:18) and promised presence (v. 20) motivate us on this mission?

-------------------------------------------------------------------

-------------------------------------------------------------------

-------------------------------------------------------------------

-------------------------------------------------------------------

Read through the following three sections on *Gospel Glimpses, Whole-Bible Connections,* and *Theological Soundings.* Then take time to consider the *Personal Implications* these sections may have for you.

## ▶ Gospel Glimpses

**FORSAKEN FOR OUR ACCEPTANCE.** On Jesus' final night a supposed friend betrayed him (Matt. 26:14–25), his three closest disciples fell asleep at their post (26:36–46), and all deserted him (26:30–35, 56). Yet the abandonment by his friends is incomparable to the abandonment by his Father. On the cross, Jesus cried out, "My God, my God, why have you forsaken me?" (27:46). This is the cry of the damned, the cry of the forsaken, the cry of one crushed under the full weight of God's holy wrath. It is the despair every one of us deserves to express forever because of our sin. Yet Jesus was forsaken so that we don't have to be. He was rejected for our acceptance; cast out for our welcome. The authentic Christian life is one that is "re-humbled" by this, time and again.

**THE GOSPEL EVENTS.** The New Testament summarizes the gospel message, "the good news," in various ways (for example, Rom. 1:1–4; 1 Cor. 15:1–5). One way is by summarizing the story of Jesus. The earliest title given to Matthew's narrative implies that the whole account was a presentation of the good news, for it is simply *"According to Matthew,"* that is, *the gospel* according to Matthew. Jesus, through his words and miracles, declared and showed the salvation he came to bring: the establishment of God's kingdom, reconciling sinners to God, and restoring all that is broken. Now through his death and resurrection, he has accomplished this salvation.

## ▶ Whole-Bible Connections

**NEW COVENANT.** Jesus explained the significance of the cup at the Last Supper in terms of a new covenant[3] (Matt. 26:28). Just as the old covenant was inaugurated with the blood of sacrifice, so too will the new covenant be, but this time with the blood of Jesus. This new covenant was promised in Jeremiah: "I will put my law within them, and I will write it on their hearts. And I will be their God, and they shall be my people.... I will forgive their iniquity, and I will remember their sin no more" (Jer. 31:33–34; see Heb. 8:7–13). Full forgiveness of sins, a restored relationship with God, and a new empowerment to obey, were all purchased for us at the cross.

**THE TORN VEIL AND OUR RETURN TO EDEN.** The garden of Eden was paradise because it was the place of God's presence. Yet when Adam and Eve rejected God, they were cast out of Eden and thereby lost their access to God's presence. A glimpse of Eden was restored in Israel's tabernacle, and later temple, where God once again dwelled with his people. To enter the temple was, in a sense, to return to Eden. Yet only the high priest could enter, and he only once a year. When Jesus died, "the curtain of the temple was torn in two, from top to bottom" (Matt. 27:51). God ripped open the symbol of separation through the sacrifice of his Son. Jesus has flung the gates of Eden wide open to all who will enter by way of his sacrifice. We now "have confidence to enter the holy places by the blood of Jesus, by the new and living way that he opened for us through the curtain, that is, through his flesh" (Heb. 10:19–20). Restored to God by faith, we now await a new heaven and a new earth—a new and better Eden—to be with God forever (Rev. 21:1–5; 22:1–5).

**THE JUDGMENT OF DEATH AND EXILE.** The earth quakes and the sky darkens at noon (Matt. 27:45, 51). God's Son is crucified. What does this mean? Centuries earlier the prophet Amos spoke about a coming day of judgment and exile for Israel. "Shall not the land tremble ... and all of it rise like the Nile and be tossed about and sink again, like the Nile of Egypt? ... I will make the sun go down at noon and darken the earth in broad daylight.... I will make it like the mourning for an only son" (Amos 8:8–10). Israel deserves this devastation for their sinful rebellion against God. So does everyone else. Yet when the earth quaked and the sky darkened at noon, the judgment didn't fall on Israel or any of us; it fell on Jesus. He came to take *our* curse, *our* punishment, *our* exile, *our* death, the hell *we* deserve. The anticipated judgment upon Israel and the world fell on Jesus in the middle of history so that all who trust him will be spared when the final judgment comes.

▶ **Theological Soundings**

**BAPTISM AND THE LORD'S SUPPER.** Baptism (Matt. 28:18–20) and the Lord's Supper (26:26–29) are two sacraments that Jesus instituted for his church to observe. Both sacraments are visible pictures of the gospel. Baptism represents one's union with Jesus in his death and resurrection (see Rom. 6:3–4), and the bread and cup of the Lord's Supper represent Jesus' body and blood given up for us on the cross (see 1 Cor. 11:23–25). Every Christian is called to be baptized and to regularly celebrate the Lord's Supper with fellow Christians.

**ATONEMENT.** Matthew highlights Jesus' innocence and righteousness in the events immediately leading up to his death (Matt. 26:59–60; 27:4, 19, 23). Jesus' righteousness clearly shows that he did not die for his own sin but for the sins of others. As the apostle Paul would later write, "For our sake he [God the Father] made him to be sin who knew no sin, so that in him we might become the righteousness of God" (2 Cor. 5:21; see Matt. 20:28).

**TRINITY.** Jesus' commission includes the directive to baptize new disciples "in the name of the Father and of the Son and of the Holy Spirit" (Matt. 28:19). Here we see the three distinct persons of the Trinity together identified as a singular "name" and therefore as constituting one God. This is not one person who manifests himself as three different entities (modalism). Nor is this referring to three separate gods (tritheism). Rather, there is one God who eternally exists as three persons (Father, Son, and Holy Spirit).

## ▶ Personal Implications

Take time to reflect on various implications of Matthew for your own life today. Additionally, consider what you have learned that might lead you to praise God, repent of sin, trust his gracious promises, and live in obedience to him. Make notes below on the personal implications for your walk with the Lord regarding the (1) *Gospel Glimpses*, (2) *Whole-Bible Connections*, (3) *Theological Soundings*, and (4) this passage as a whole.

### 1. Gospel Glimpses

### 2. Whole-Bible Connections

## 3. Theological Soundings

## 4. Matthew 26–28

> ### As You Finish This Unit . . .

Take a moment now to ask for the Lord's blessing and help as you continue in this study of Matthew. And take a moment also to look back through this unit of study, to reflect on a few key things that the Lord may be teaching you—and perhaps to highlight and underline these things to review again in the future.

### Definitions

[1] **Passover** – An annual Israelite festival commemorating God's final plague on the Egyptians, which led to the exodus. In this final plague, the Lord "passed over" the houses of those who spread the blood of a lamb on the doorposts of their homes (Exodus 12). Those who did not obey this command suffered the death of their firstborn.

[2] **Crucifixion** – A means of execution in which the person was fastened, by ropes or nails, to a crossbeam that was then raised and attached to a vertical beam, forming a cross. The process was designed to maximize pain and humiliation, and to serve as a deterrent for other offenders.

[3] **Covenant** – A binding agreement between two parties in a formal relationship. The OT is more properly understood as the old covenant, meaning the state of agreement established between God and his people prior to the coming of Jesus Christ and the establishment of the new covenant (NT).

# WEEK 12: SUMMARY AND CONCLUSION

We will draw this study to a close by summarizing the big picture of God's message through Matthew as a whole. Then we will consider several questions in order to reflect on what we have seen throughout the entirety of Matthew.

## The Big Picture of Matthew

From the outset, Matthew presents Jesus as the long-awaited King who inaugurates the kingdom of heaven. In other words, Jesus came to reestablish God's rule and restore all that is broken in this world. Matthew broadly moves his narrative along chronological lines, but he also groups various aspects of Jesus' life and ministry together according to similar themes. He shows us Jesus' authoritative teaching (Matthew 5–7), his powerful ministry (Matthew 8–9), and his disciples' mission (Matthew 10). We also heard his teaching on the kingdom (Matthew 13), his new community (Matthew 18), and the trials to expect as we await his return (Matthew 24–25).

As his own name indicates, Jesus came to "save his people from their sins" (1:21), a salvation he accomplished through his death as he gave his life as "a ransom for many" (20:28). In the end, Jesus is the resurrected King who commissions his people to make more disciples by preaching the good news of his kingdom to all nations (Matt. 24:14; 28:18–20).

## Gospel Glimpses

Matthew expresses God's grace for sinners in various ways throughout the details of this gospel story. From the beginning we see notorious sinners included in Christ's lineage. Throughout his ministry he was attracted to the broken, the outcast, and the poor in spirit. He gives health to the sick, sight to the blind, freedom to the demon-oppressed, food to the hungry, and forgiveness to the guilty. When he saw the crowds, he had compassion. When he saw the weary, he offered rest. Most of all, when he saw humanity in all our sinfulness and separation from God, he came to take our sins upon himself at the cross. He "came not to be served but to serve, and to give his life as a ransom for many" (20:28). The gospel reminds us that we do not first serve God. His service to us in the gospel comes first and remains primary.

How has Matthew clarified, changed, or deepened your understanding of the gospel?

What are a few particular passages or themes in Matthew that led you to have a fresh understanding and grasp of the gospel? How do these give you a fresh grasp of God's grace to you in the gospel?

## Whole-Bible Connections

From the opening genealogy, Matthew sets the story of Jesus in the context of the ongoing story of the Old Testament. He is the one through whom God would fulfill the central promises of the Old Testament—promises to bless all nations and restore all things through a coming Davidic king. Jesus announces the dawning of this kingdom and then displays its presence through healing sickness, calming storms, subduing demons, and forgiving sins.

Jesus' identity is also robustly filled out from the Old Testament, for Matthew presents him as the Son of Abraham, the Son of David, and the long-awaited Messiah. He is greater than the temple, greater than Jonah, and greater than Solomon. He is the Prophet like Moses, the Lord of the Sabbath, and the ultimate Passover sacrifice. He is the exalted Son of Man and the beloved Son of God. He is the compassionate Shepherd of the sheep and the self-sacrificing suffering Servant. He is Immanuel and the great I AM. In these ways and others, we see that he did not come to abolish the Old Testament Scriptures but to fulfill them.

What connections to Old Testament promises, themes, or expectations were new to you in this study?

How has this study of Matthew filled out your understanding of the biblical storyline of redemption?

Have any of Matthew's passages or themes expanded your understanding of how the Old and New Testaments are connected?

## Theological Soundings

Matthew's Gospel richly informs our theology. It shows us the Trinity (Father, Son, and Holy Spirit) and puts a spotlight on Jesus' nature (his humanity and deity) and his work (his obedient life, substitutionary death, victorious resurrection, and future glorious return). It also clarifies and fills out our understanding of the doctrines of God's sovereignty and human responsibility, human sin and eternal judgment, grace and salvation, the kingdom of God and the mission of the church, and the future return of Jesus.

Has your theology shifted in minor or major ways during the course of studying Matthew? How so?

How has your understanding of the nature and character of God been deepened throughout this study?

How does Matthew contribute to our understanding of who Jesus is and what he accomplished through his life, death, and resurrection?

What, specifically, does Matthew teach us about what it means to be a Christian?